CW00833774

Why Do the Innocent Suffer?

Michael R. Saia

PRESS

Copyright © 2014 by Michael R. Saia

Why Do the Innocent Suffer?
by Michael R. Saia

Available from:
Upbuilders International
Ph: 425-672-8708
www.upbuilders.com

Printed in the United States of America

Library of Congress Control Number:
ISBN 9781629523453

All rights reserved solely by the author. The author guarantees all contents are original and do not infringe upon the legal rights of any other person or work. No part of this book may be reproduced in any form without the permission of the author. The views expressed in this book are not necessarily those of the publisher.

Unless otherwise indicated, Bible quotations are taken from the New American Standard Bible. Copyright © 1977 by the Lockman Foundation.

The SymbolGreekII & NewJerusalem fonts used in this work are available from Linguist's Software, Inc. P.O. Box 580, Edmonds, WA 98020-0580, USA. Tel (425)-775-1130
www.linguistsoftware.com.

www.xulonpress.com

To order additional copies, call 1-866-909-2665

Acknowledgements

It would be hard to thank all of the people who contributed to my thinking about the important subject of suffering. But I must thank at least a few of them who have played an important role in the writing and publishing of *Why Do the Innocent Suffer?*

Thanks, Rohan and Paula, for your friendship, and for your practical help with the writing and publishing of this book. God will not forget your labor of love or your reward.

Thank you, July, for your suggestions and for your help with the editing of this book.

Thank you, Roger, for the use of your photograph on the cover.

Thanks, Floyd, for stimulating my thinking on this important subject during my School of Evangelism in Lausanne.

Thanks so much, Dean, for your encouragement, your fellowship, and your endorsement.

Thank you, Peter, for your support, your endorsement, and your enthusiasm for a Gospel that vindicates the justice and love of our Heavenly Father.

Thanks, Carol, for your encouragement and support, both as my wife, and as a diligent editor.

Thanks most of all to You, Lord, for Your justice, Your love, and for helping me to understand that You are never responsible for the suffering of any innocent person.

Table of Contents

Introduction

Immediately following the horrific events of September 11, 2001, the media were awash in interviews with people asking about suffering and God's relationship to the presence of evil in the world. Then, when a tsunami struck Indonesia and the Indian ocean in 2004, killing more than a quarter million people, many questioned how the Christian concept of a good God squares with the reality of natural disasters. Then another tsunami killed over 19,000 in Japan, devastating the country and wiping whole villages into the sea. Multiple school shootings, and a slaughter of innocent people in a Colorado theatre prompted the questions all over again. Hurricane Sandy struck, affecting millions on the East Coast of the US. Then the murder of twenty children and six adults in a school in Connecticut forced the problem of evil and suffering in our faces again. Then there were the Boston Marathon bombings. It seems every time people turn around they are confronted with the problem of evil. In light of all this suffering, questions about God's goodness are unavoidable, while intellectually-satisfying, biblical answers to the problem seem to be in short supply.

With the problem of suffering, the stakes are the highest they can be. If people are convinced God is truly good, in spite of the presence of pain in the world, they can live in relationship with Him, undisturbed by any evil they may encounter. But if God's goodness and justice are suspect, then either consciously or subconsciously people will have problems relating to God, because they must always question whether or not they can fully trust God's character. Since knowing God is the definition of eternal life,[1] then an understanding of suffering can mean the difference between eternal life and eternal death to those asking the question.

---

[1] John 17:3.

God's character needs to be justified in the minds of those who have questions about why innocent people can suffer. Though the Bible declares, "The Lord is just in all his ways, and kind in all his deeds,"[2] if a person is not convinced in his mind this is true, it will be difficult for the person to trust God with his whole heart and life. Since some of the theological and philosophical views of God promoted in the Church today either imply or directly state God is unjust in His treatment of the innocent, it is not surprising many Christians have doubts about the goodness and justice of God.

Good answers will not make suffering disappear, nor will they make it hurt any less. But if a person is convinced God is not responsible for the innocent suffering, it allows the person to separate the subjects of God and suffering in his thinking. The Bible tells us, "The spirit of a man can endure his sickness, but a broken spirit who can bear?"[3] Suffering is bad enough in itself, but if you think God is behind your suffering, you not only have the suffering to deal with, but also the nagging suspicion God is against you. This is not true, of course, but some theologies teach God is either directly or indirectly responsible for the presence of evil in the universe. If the world is against you, and you also think God secretly wants you to suffer, then who can help you with the pain?

Our view of God's nature and character influences how we understand suffering, and God's relationship to it. Does God's existence include a moral aspect, or only power and some kind of fixed plan for the world? Is God responsible to live according to a law, such as the law of love, or is He free to do whatever He wants in the universe? Does God choose to do something because it is right, or is it right because He chose to do it?

When people assume God's actions relative to suffering are significant, they are presupposing God must live according to some kind of moral law. This means His actions can be judged by some kind of moral standard. Yet when it comes to His actions in general, they often assume God can just do whatever He wants, and whatever He does will be right. This means His actions cannot

---

[2] Psalm 145:17.
[3] Proverbs 18:14.

be judged by any moral standard. These two views cannot both be correct.

How much God respects the free will of man, and other moral beings, is another factor affecting our thinking about why innocent people can suffer. If God does not need to consider how His actions will affect other free-will beings, then He can do whatever He wants with impunity. In that case, we would have to ask, "Then why doesn't God just stop all suffering in the world?" But if God respects man's freedom and significance, then He cannot simply do anything He wants without harming those He made in His own image. Again, the two views are mutually exclusive, and the way one views God's treatment of free-will beings determines what we will think of God's relationship to suffering.

Some people think it is entirely possible to separate what they believe from the logical conclusions of those beliefs. They convince themselves their presuppositions need not lead to any logical or practical consequences in the world. Either that, or they hold assumptions and conclusions that are mutually inconsistent, but accept both as true simultaneously. Their hearts and minds reach different conclusions about God's goodness, but they accept both as true and try to live with the tension. A friend of mine calls this the "great disconnect."

This discrepancy was dramatically illustrated in the life of a Christian politician in the United States. When he was asked about his position on whether abortion was permissible in cases of rape, his answer was if a baby exists because of a rape, then it is the will of God the baby exist. Sadly, many Christians will accept this kind of faulty reasoning without taking it to its logical conclusion. But the national press did not miss the point. Within 24 hours, the news programs were filled with reports of how this politician believes it is God's will if a woman is raped. Of course, this was not what he intended to communicate, but it is the logical conclusion of his statement. If God wanted the baby to exist, and the baby would be conceived through an act of rape, then it also had to be His will that the woman be raped. Unfortunately, many Christians do not even think about how their beliefs work out logically to specific conclusions. In this case, the politician's careless remark probably cost him the election.

9

Sometimes it is necessary to change our understanding about God and His ways when our old belief system does not agree with the Bible and good logic. These adjustments are not easy, since our emotional comfort often depends on our concept of God. It is far easier to ignore our logical fallacies, and stop listening to the Scriptures, than to change how we view Him. The problem with this avoidance is we may ultimately hold God responsible for situations in the world that are not His fault. For some people, blaming God for the presence of evil in the world seems easier than changing their ideas about Him.

"The foolishness of man subverts his way, and his heart rages against the Lord."[4] This proverb is demonstrated in the lives of countless people, maybe even on a daily basis. For example, a man gets drunk, runs his car into a tree, and ends up in the hospital. And what does he ask, lying in the hospital with two broken legs? "Oh God, why did you do this to me?" Or he might be a little less obvious in his accusation of God, asking, "God, why did You allow this to happen to me?" Either way, he subverts his own way, but his heart rages against God, blaming the Lord for his own foolishness.

This proverb could be a metaphor for the whole human race. We, in our foolishness and rebellion against God, have subverted our way, corrupting our own lives and the entire creation. But instead of accepting our own responsibility, our hearts rage against God, asking why He did this, or in our more philosophical moments, questioning how the Lord could have "allowed" this to happen.

The situation is trickier, though, when the suffering is not obviously the result of a person's own choices. What about the baby who is born deformed, the woman who is raped, the child who is killed in a war, or the victim of a random, drive-by shooting? These people were not subverting their ways, and yet they suffered. When there does not appear to be a direct connection between the person's choices and their suffering, the question of God's involvement in the situation becomes more complicated, and also more troubling. If God could have stopped the suffering, then why did He not do so?

---

[4] Proverbs 19:3.

The church is in desperate need of widespread teaching on suffering from an intellectually-satisfying, and truly biblical standpoint. There are good answers for this question, but it is easier to spout clichés than to apply our hearts and minds to the Scriptures for a solution. Telling people, "God has everything under control," or "Everything that happens is the will of God," or "Everything works out for the best" simply will not suffice when someone is in serious pain. Rather than answering the question, these explanations might only make it more difficult for the suffering person to turn to God for help. Logical, biblical answers are the only remedy for a mind troubled by the question of suffering.

Just a few years ago, it was common to hear either no instruction about the problem of evil from the pulpit, or explanations that ultimately held God responsible for all the suffering in the world. More recently, it has been encouraging to hear people grappling with the subject, trying to provide real answers for their congregations. There have also been more books, articles, and videos offering better information to the Body of Christ. What we need is a whole generation of Christians armed with reasonable, biblical explanations for the innocent suffering. That way, we can prepare the next generation of believers, arming their minds and hearts to deal philosophically, theologically, and practically with this vital subject. Eventually, then, we may have a body of believers who can answer the question of the innocent suffering logically, and who can effectively minister to those in painful situations without slandering the goodness and justice of God.

Logical, biblical instruction on suffering is also the best way to be practically prepared to deal with the reality of evil and pain in our own lives. If we can arm ourselves with answers to the problem of pain before we suffer, we will find it easier to refrain from blaming God when we do suffer. When we know the truth about God's relationship to pain and evil, our minds can rest in the midst of suffering. Convinced that God loves us, and is not the cause of our suffering, we can trust He will help us in every way He can.

Chapter 1

The Problem of Evil

"Why do the innocent suffer?" is probably one of the most important questions a person can ask, perhaps apart from whether or not there is a God. But since most people who ask the question are already assuming there is a God, the suffering of the innocent takes very high priority.

Even if it is not the most important question, it is definitely one of the topics most frequently encountered during evangelism. But people have different reasons for asking the question. Some people really want an answer, because they are trying to determine if they can trust the God of the Bible with their lives. Others simply want to avoid God altogether, and so attempt to use the question as a distraction. Regardless of the person's motives, though, if the question is asked, it deserves serious attention. Any person who asks the question is a being made in the image of God, and as such they have a right to question whether or not God's character is trustworthy.

"The answer to why the innocent suffer is very simple," the speaker announced boldly. "The unbeliever does not have the right to ask the question, so he does not deserve an answer." I was attending an apologetics seminar at a church near my home to see how other Christians are handling apologetics with this generation. Needless to say, I was more than amazed a follower of Christ would think of treating an unbeliever with such disrespect, disdain, and dismissal. He then went on to say as Christians we should know we are not to question the justice of God, so the whole problem of the innocent suffering, for both the unbeliever and the believer, is an irrelevant topic. I found the conference unhelpful in general, and completely useless with regard to suffering, a topic God treats as extremely important in His Word.

God's first written communication to man may have been about the suffering of an innocent person.[5] As far as when the texts of our current Bible were written, it is likely the Book of Job was the first chronologically.[6] If so, this indicates how important the subject of suffering must be to God and to human beings.

Three Little Words

The biggest problem in the universe, the problem of evil, is often expressed in some of the shortest phrases. For humans, it can even be expressed in just three, one-syllable words, "Why me, God?" The simplicity with which this question can be asked does not diminish the significance of the issue. In fact, each word of the question reveals a different, vital aspect of the problem.

"Why?" This question by itself is the root of the entire puzzle. Why does evil exist? Where does evil come from? What is its nature? When confronted with something that tears apart the very fabric of reality, and produces such profound pain, the response is natural, immediate, and unavoidable. We must ask, "Why?"

But the evil in the universe is not just a generalization. When evil happens, it affects us as individuals. We do not see cats, dogs, horses, or rabbits asking why there is suffering, pain, and destruction in the world. *We* ask the question, because we, as beings made in the image of God, must ask the question, given the state of the creation. Thus, the second word in the query need not be an expression of self-pity, though it might contain elements of that sentiment.

---

[5] Please see Chapter 5 for an expanded explanation of the suffering of Job.

[6] Galatians 3:8 states "The Scriptures preached the Gospel to Abraham," implying there were some writings either prior to or during Abraham's lifetime. These may have been used as a basis for some of the books of Moses, but since these prior writings were not preserved, it is impossible to tell if there were any documents prior to Job. Internal evidence does indicate, however, that Job was probably written prior to the writings of Moses. Any good, conservative introduction to the Old Testament should include this evidence.

THE PROBLEM OF EVIL

When we ask, "Why me?" we are most often questioning the injustice of the suffering. "Why am I suffering, when I didn't do anything to deserve this?" As moral beings, we are forced to ask why innocent people can suffer. Our innate sense of morality, of right and wrong, of intuitive moral law, instinctively responds to the injustice of an innocent being's suffering. When we suffer as innocent parties, we are constrained to ask, "Why me?"

The third word, "God," introduces the most difficult questions of all. "How could God have let evil come into being? Why does He allow it to continue? If He could create every atom of the entire universe, couldn't He stop evil from beginning? If He is still so powerful, then why can't He make evil go away? Or if He can't eliminate evil, can't He just take away the negative consequences?" Some have even proposed evil is the will of God, because in some way the universe will be a better place *with* evil, than *without* it. As shocking as this idea may be to some, this teaching is actually quite common in the church today.[7]

They are three little words, and yet three very big words. "Why me, God?" embodies the essence of the problem of evil, and leads us to look for answers to one of life's biggest questions.

Who Are the Innocent?

"I don't understand the question," the student remarked. "You say the innocent can suffer, but I was under the impression that all have sinned, and there are no innocent parties. So how can innocent people suffer? What do you mean by the word 'innocent'?"

This was a great question, and frankly, once I heard it, I was surprised it had never come up before. When asking, "Why do the innocent suffer?" it is important to establish who the "innocent" are. If there are no innocent parties, then the question of the "innocent" suffering would be irrelevant.[8]

Since we have all rebelled against God, one would assume there really are no innocent parties, with perhaps the exception

---

[7] Please see Chapter 2 for a discussion on the idea of the necessity of evil.
[8] As it is in Hinduism, which will be discussed in Chapter 2.

of unborn children and young babies. Referring to Jacob and Esau, Paul the Apostle said, "...though the twins were not yet born, and had not done anything good or bad...." So Paul, at least, believed unborn children are truly innocent. But all humans eventually go astray,[9] rebelling against the law of God from a very young age. Thus, how can anyone claim innocence in light of any suffering he might endure?

Oddly, when Christians consider suffering, they seem to apply a standard of guilt and innocence they do not use in any other sphere of our society. When they say a person is innocent of murder, they mean the person has not murdered anyone. They do not assume because a person has rebelled against God in other ways, that the person is therefore guilty of murder as well.[10] They distinguish between the choices a person makes, recognizing him as guilty of some crimes, but innocent of others. If a person is wrongly convicted of murder, then they say he was "innocent" of murder.

It is in this same way the "innocent" can suffer. The person is innocent with respect to any particular choices that could have brought about the suffering, but not in the sense he has never committed any sins at all (babies being the exception, of course). Thus, if a person is hit in a drive-by shooting, there may have been nothing the person did to deserve being shot, even though the

---

[9] This is in the statistical sense, of course, since there are those rare cases listed in the Scriptures of people who appear to have been blameless in keeping the law—Enoch, Zacharias and Elizabeth.

[10] I have heard people quote the book of James to support the idea that anyone who commits any sin is guilty of every sin, but that is not what James says. If we read the words carefully, we see James is saying if we commit any sin, we are transgressors of the law, but not that if we commit any sin, we have committed every sin. "But if you show partiality, you are committing sin and are convicted by the law as transgressors. For whoever keeps the whole law and yet stumbles in one point, he has become guilty of all. For He who said, 'Do not commit adultery,' also said, 'Do not commit murder.' Now if you do not commit adultery, but do commit murder, you have become a transgressor of the law." James 2:9-11. Note that James does not say, "You have become a murderer," but rather, "You have become a transgressor of the law." Since the whole law boils down to one precept—love—then if a person commits any sin, he has broken the whole law because he failed to love. But this does not mean if a person commits adultery he is also a murderer.

person was not innocent in the sense he had never sinned. So the word "innocent" in "Why do the innocent suffer?" is restricted to being innocent with respect to the particular suffering the person is experiencing.

David Hume and the Problem of Evil

The basic question of the problem of evil is often presented as, "If God is loving, and all-powerful, then why doesn't He just stop all the suffering? Better yet, why didn't He just prevent it from happening in the first place?"

This format is similar to, or perhaps even derived from, an argument used by David Hume in his *Dialogues Concerning Natural Religion*, Part 10. It is quite common to hear college students who have studied philosophy present the question following Hume's pattern.

The Scottish philosopher[11] presents his argument in this way:

"Is he willing to prevent evil, but not able? Then he is impotent.
Is he able but not willing? Then he is malevolent.
Is he both able and willing? Whence then is evil?"[12]

Basically he is questioning whether the Christian God, who is supposed to be all powerful (omnipotent), and also all loving, could allow evil to exist, given those two qualities. If God is powerful enough to stop evil, but does not, then He must not be loving. If God is loving, and willing to stop evil, then He must not have enough power to do it. If He is both powerful and loving, Hume reasons, then evil should not exist in the universe.

---

[11] 1711-1776.

[12] Philo, one of the speakers in the Dialogues, speaking to Cleanthes, is supposedly quoting the Greek philosopher Epicurus (B.C. 341-270), whose argument was more like: "Is God willing to prevent evil, but not able? Then he is not omnipotent. Is he able, but not willing? Then he is malevolent. Is he both able and willing? Then whence cometh evil? Is he neither able nor willing? Then why call him God?" The argument is basically the same in form, though, so for our purposes, we will use Hume's presentation.

There are many difficulties with Hume's presentation, but since the problem of evil is so important, he should probably be given wide latitude. Some distinctions are worth noting, though, since the distinctions will be useful to later discussions.

Without carefully defining his words, such as "able," "impotent," "malevolent," "willing," and "evil," (basically all the important words in the argument), the argument becomes more emotional than philosophical. This is permissible, though, since the subject of suffering is an emotional one.

First, a distinction that will be very useful later is the different uses of the word "able." There are two ways to define an ability— metaphysical,[13] or moral. I may well be "able" to sell you my house for one dollar, but I am not "able" to do so, for the sake of my family. A similar comparison would be the Bible's assertion God "can" do all things, but God "cannot" lie. This distinction is not trivial, but describes the important difference between the *power* to do something, on the one hand, and the *moral freedom* to do something on the other.

What does it mean, then, for God to be "able" to stop evil? Since the word "able" is linked verbally and logically to the word "impotent" in Hume's argument, I assume he is speaking metaphysically—talking about God's power. That is, maybe God does not have the power to stop evil. Hume's argument ignores the distinction between these two uses of the word "able." Just as I am both "able" and not "able" to sell my house for one dollar, so God might be "able" (has the power) but not be "able" (morally free) to stop evil. In this case, though, Hume appears to be referring strictly to God's power, and not His morality.

Second, it is entirely possible for a being to be unable to stop evil, and yet not be completely "impotent" (having no power at all). This is the case for human beings. We have power to do many things, but stopping all evil is not within our abilities. Since Hume

---

[13] Metaphysics deals with being, whereas morals deal with choices. One of my metaphysical characteristics is my brown eyes. I did not choose them. They are part of my being. My kindness, on the other hand, would be a moral quality. I choose whether or not to be kind. Power to create would be one of God's metaphysical qualities (attributes), whereas His justice would be one of His moral qualities.

is defining "impotent" as "not able to prevent evil," then his denial of God's omnipotence rests on his definition of "able" as metaphysical power.

Third, one might ask whether or not there could be good reasons for not choosing to stop evil, even if one is able. Defining "malevolent" only as "able, but not willing" overlooks any good reasons a moral being might have to withhold activity. What if relieving the world of all evil would produce greater harm than allowing it to continue? If the only way to stop all evil is to remove all free will, then the cure would be worse than the problem. In that case, being unwilling should be considered benevolent rather than malevolent.

Again, if being "malevolent" means only not stopping evil when one could have, then the definition includes only evil by omission, and not by commission, which is a very limited definition of the word. If God were truly malevolent, both by omission and commission, then there would be no reason to argue about why God does not stop evil. In that case, it might be more pertinent to discuss whether or not God is the author of all suffering.

Fourth, being "willing" does not always imply a person is free, morally, to do something he might want to do. For example, if a driver is caught speeding, he should be given a ticket for his infraction of the traffic laws. If there are extenuating circumstances, the officer may desire to forego the speeding ticket, but not be morally free to do so. Being "willing" to do something is not the same as being morally free to do it.

This same principle is evident in child training. There are times when a parent does not want to discipline the child, but knows if the greatest good is going to result in the child's life, the parent must fulfill the responsibility to discipline. God also experiences this internal conflict when He must discipline us. Jeremiah says of God, "For He does not afflict willingly."[14] Thus, there are times when God must afflict people, though He does not want to do it.

Fifth, the word "evil" is not carefully defined, so it is unclear if Hume is referring to choices, or the detrimental results of choices, or both. Whether or not God is free to stop a person from sinning is

---

[14] Lamentations 33:3.

very different from allowing a person to sin while preventing any consequences. Both definitions are used in the Bible, where people are recorded as doing evil (sinning), and God is described as bringing "evil" (calamity, destruction) on them for their sin. For the sake of the argument, though, it is probably best to consider Hume's word as representing both the commission and consequences of evil, since both kinds of evil are problems in a universe where God is both powerful and loving.

Notice, too, Hume's entire argument assumes God can be judged by the same principles of justice we would understand as applicable to human beings. This is not a problem, however, since the Bible describes people as using this kind of reasoning with God. Abraham asked, "Shall not the Judge of all the earth deal justly?"[15] He expected God to at least live according to the moral standards he perceived as a human being. God did not fault Abraham for this, but reasoned with him on this basis for the preservation of Sodom and Gomorrah.[16]

Though Hume's argument has its difficulties, it does express the way many people think about the problem of evil. If God is both loving and powerful, how can evil exist?

Possible Sources of Evil

Though the problem of evil is complex, and sometimes confusing, there are only a few possible sources for the origin of evil.

First, evil could have existed forever, as a kind of "evil opposite" of God. This view is common in some schools of Zoroastrianism, where Ahura Mazda, the "good" god, has co-

---

[15] Genesis 18:25.

[16] Many people assume Abraham's prayer was not answered because Sodom and Gomorrah were destroyed. But what did Abraham request? He asked that the righteous not be destroyed with the wicked. He also asked that the city not be destroyed based on the presence of righteous inhabitants. Since 1) the righteous (Lot and his family) were not in Sodom when it was destroyed, and 2) Lot and his family were spared, and 3) Zoar, the city where they fled, was also spared, then all of Abraham's requests were granted. Abraham even received more than he asked for, since God did not destroy Zoar based on the presence of three righteous people. He did not require ten, as agreed upon with Abraham.

existed for all eternity with Angra Mainyu, the "evil" god.[17] Other schools view Ahura Mazda as creating two other "spirits," one evil (Spento-Mainyu) and one good (Angro Mainyu), and these two are in opposition before and in the creation.[18] Thus, there is a kind of duality in god, with both good and evil forces existing together for all eternity. Unlike Greek dualism, though, where the physical and spiritual are in opposition, in this system the conflict is between two spiritual forces—one good, and the other evil.[19]

In this case it is not necessary to ask how evil originated, since it had no beginning. But there is also no solution for the problem of evil, since evil is simply part of what is, and what has always been, and possibly what will always be.[20] As with many other monistic systems, it is sometimes difficult to tell how human good and evil relates to the spiritual forces of good and evil in the universe. Hinduism, though inconsistent within its own system, seems somewhat clearer than the Zoroastrian worldview.[21]

Some Christians hold a view similar to this, with evil as a force equal to God, but opposing Him. Identifying this force with the biblical personage of Satan, or the Devil, they propose two forces, one good and one evil, struggling with each other in human history. This is unbiblical, of course, since Satan is a finite, created, personal, spiritual being, and not an evil force equal to God.

Second, God could have created evil. There are a couple of ways to view this possibility. One way is that God created some kind of force we identify as "evil" and released it in the world. This is the direct approach. Most Christians would reject this idea outright, understanding a good God would not create something evil and then subject human beings to its onslaught.

---

[17] Some schools teach that Ahura Mazda created Angra Mainyu, but that would mean evil is finite, and created, and would fall under one of the other categories.
[18] http://www.farvardyn.com/zoroaster3.php.
[19] C. S. Lewis discusses the impossibility of an eternally-existing, evil being in his essay "God and Evil" in his book *God in the Dock: Essays in Theology and Ethics*.
[20] Some Zoroastrians teach that Ahura Mazda will eventually defeat Angra Mainyu, placing it "underground," however that works, but that makes little difference to how evil is described in the whole system.
[21] The Hindu view of suffering is discussed further in Chapter 2.

But there is another way Christians present this same idea, obscuring the dark reality with a fancy theological cloak. "Everything that happens is the will of God," they teach. "God planned the history of the world, so if evil happens, then it must somehow be His will, though we don't know why He did it."

Those who are not so bold as to blame God for evil will sometimes soften the impact of the doctrine with statements like, "Well, before God created, He knew evil would exist. This is not His fault, though. He just saw we would rebel against Him. But He chose to create us anyway, knowing what would happen. We don't know how to square this with the justice of God, but it's not our place to question His choices."

Either way, they are saying God wanted evil to exist, for some reason unknown to us, and we must simply accept its presence in the world.[22]

Third, evil could be the "creation" of finite beings. When a finite being makes a choice, that decision brings about consequences in the universe. But we not only create consequences in the universe by our choices, we also create the choices themselves. Our free will originates choices that never existed before, so in a sense, our free will "creates" our choices. Since our will is part of what we are as beings made in the image of God, then you could say we create our own choices, and as a result, create the consequences of those choices.

Using this definition, evil is not a thing, but rather consists of the rebellious choices of finite beings. The destructive consequences of those bad choices could also be spoken of as part of the evil in the world. The rebellious choices of finite beings (human and spiritual), together with the consequences of those choices, could be used as a definition of "evil." In this view, then, evil would have a finite source, and be finite in scope.

---

[22] There is an extended discussion of this viewpoint in Chapter 2.

Chapter 2

Inadequate Answers

Since every philosophy is believed by humans who can suffer, every philosophy must offer some explanation for the presence of pain in the world.[23] In their philosophies, people either believe there is something wrong with the world, or the world is exactly as it should be. People who think something is wrong with the world want to know what went wrong, who might be responsible, and whether or not the situation can be remedied. For those who think the world is as it should be, the question of evil cannot even be asked, because there is no standard by which to determine the world should be different from what it is.

The proposed answers fall into three logical categories—naturalistic, monistic, or Christian. This is because either 1) there is no God, and only matter and energy exist, as in naturalism, or 2) god is an infinite, impersonal force, as in Hinduism, or 3) God is infinite and personal, as in the Judeo-Christian framework. Since the presuppositions of the various philosophical systems determine which conclusions they can and cannot reach, knowing where the

---

[23] I first heard the approach of explaining the inadequate answers of various non-Christian philosophies in a lecture by Floyd McClung in my School of Evangelism in Lausanne, Switzerland in 1972. The explanations of the inadequate answers are mine, but the general idea of dealing with them before presenting the Christian answer was introduced to me in those classes. I am not sure if this approach is original to McClung, but I am grateful I heard it, and find it very helpful in discussing the problem of evil. It is similar to C. S. Lewis's method of first presenting what a word does not mean before giving the real definition.

systems start is crucial to knowing how they will handle the topic of suffering.

In discussing any philosophy, it is good to remember philosophies and theologies are believed by human beings made in the image of God. As such, the people should be respected and treated with dignity and love. Confronting a false idea is one thing, but attacking a person is something else—something that should not be part of our lives as followers of Christ. When Peter admonishes us to be "ready to make a defense to everyone who asks you to give an account for the hope that is in you," he then adds *how* it should be done—"with gentleness and reverence."[24] We should always be careful if we reject a false idea, that we do not at the same time reject the person who believes it.

Humanism

There are many definitions for the word "humanism," but what we are going to address here could be called, more technically, "atheistic, naturalistic, evolutionary humanism." The position is atheistic because it proposes there is nothing "above" matter and energy, or supernatural, such as God, angels, demons, etc. It is naturalistic because it assumes there are only natural causes in a completely closed system[25] of accidental cause and effect events. Since these natural causes are the only explanation for the existence for all living creatures, then naturalistic evolution is assumed to be the only possible process to explain the existence of human beings. Lastly, since the human brain is the most evolved material in the universe,[26] man is limited to his own finite intelligence to explain his own existence, meaning, and place in the universe.

---

[24] I Peter 3:15.

[25] Naturalism is a closed system because it assumes there is nothing other than natural causes that can operate in the system or affect it. The Christian worldview is an open system, because it presupposes the natural causes in the universe can be affected by the supernatural.

[26] Of course, this is an assumption the evolutionist makes without any empirical evidence. There is no way to know if more complex material exists somewhere else in the universe.

When the humanist tries to answer the question, "Why do the innocent suffer?" he is immediately stepping out of his own philosophical framework, and into the Christian worldview. First, since the humanist cannot establish absolute right and wrong with his finite mind, then he cannot establish true innocence or guilt. Second, since suffering is simply part of the process of evolution through natural selection and survival of the fit, then suffering cannot be said to be wrong. Third, by asking the question, the humanist has admitted there are issues in a human being's life that go far beyond evolutionary theory. Just using the word "why" assumes there might be some kind of meaning to what is happening in the universe. If everything is simply a series of accidents happening because of the natural causes in matter and energy, then there can be no purpose for anything that happens. Thus, asking "why" is irrelevant for the humanist, because it is forbidden by his presuppositions.

As far as vocabulary is concerned, the humanist must borrow from the Christian worldview even to ask the question "Why do the innocent suffer?" The concepts of meaning (why) and morality (innocent) and empathy (suffer) are completely foreign to humanist philosophy. For a creature that has evolved by accident, there is no meaning, so there is no "why." Since the finite human mind cannot establish absolute morality, then there can be no "guilty" or "innocent." And since suffering is necessary for evolution to operate, then suffering should not elicit any empathetic reaction in other humans.

Once, when I was waiting in line for a prescription, my pharmacist began discussing evolution and creation with me. He was taking the evolutionary position. After I received my prescription, and turned toward the door to leave, the pharmacist called out after me, "What about the spotted owl?"

"Well," I answered, "if the owl cannot withstand the onslaught of the human species, then it is not fit to survive, and it deserves to go extinct." I could see from the pharmacist's face he was not expecting this response. He was probably expecting me to react intuitively as a human being, and have some kind of compassion for the bird. But if evolution is true, as he was asserting, then humans, as evolved beings, are accidents too, and if the owl cannot survive as a species, then "tough luck," as they say. If evolution is true, then compassion cannot be part of any animal's behavior, including the human animal. A Christian has a basis in the biblical worldview to make efforts to preserve a species God created to His glory. An evolutionist has no reason in his philosophy to preserve any species.[27]

Now the humanist, as a human being, has the right to ask questions about the problem of evil. As a human being, he intuitively understands there is something wrong with the abuse of an innocent child. But his philosophy is not sufficient to formulate the pertinent question, and so he must borrow from the Christian system and vocabulary to ask the question at all. Still, as a human being, the humanist deserves a satisfying answer. He simply will not find it within his own philosophical framework.

When the humanist asks the question, he is usually responding to something he has heard from the Christian worldview. If God made everything, as Christians claim, then He must also be the source of evil. Why would anyone want to have a relationship with a God who makes a world like this where innocent people suffer so frequently and severely? This reaction is understandable, but it is not within the scope of the humanist's worldview to either ask the question, or offer some kind of answer.

Nihilism

Nihilism,[28] the idea that everything is meaningless, is a logical extension of humanism. Since the humanist cannot establish the absolutes necessary to conclude meaning for any finite thing in the universe, the only conclusion he can make is that everything has no meaning.

---

[27] It might be good to note, too, that helping other species so our species will be preserved is also not admissible in evolutionary theory. There is no system of values in evolution to say that any particular species should be preserved over another—not even the human species.

[28] From the Latin word for "nothing."

As with other philosophical conclusions of humanism (absolute skepticism,[29] solipsism,[30] existentialism,[31] etc.), the idea everything is meaningless may be interesting to contemplate, but it is impossible to live. People do not treat their own existence, their relationships with other people, or the objective reality around them as if they were meaningless. While it is better they react intuitively as human beings, treating themselves and others as if they have some kind of significance, it is still inconsistent with their philosophical assumptions if they are nihilists. They can assume whatever they want about the nature of reality, but they are forced by that same reality to react as if it has real meaning.

For example, when a nihilist is in pain, he usually does not say to himself, "Now this pain is meaningless, just as I am meaningless. Doctors are meaningless, treatment is meaningless, and health is meaningless. There is therefore no reason to go to the meaningless doctor to have meaningless treatment to relieve my meaningless pain. So I will not go to the doctor." But what does the nihilist do? He goes to the doctor because somehow his pain *seems* significant, even though his philosophy tells him it should not be. There would probably be far fewer nihilists if they were all consistent with their philosophy. (From our Christian perspective, though, we are happy they are inconsistent, and go to the doctor to alleviate their maladies.)

So, while nihilism is logically consistent within the philosophical framework of humanism, it is still impossible for the nihilist to live consistently with objective reality. He may claim everything, including suffering, is meaningless, but he cannot live that way.

---

[29] Absolute skepticism - the idea that any conclusion of a finite mind must be questionable, because the finite mind cannot construct the absolutes necessary to establish absolute truth.

[30] Solipsism - the idea that a person can only be sure of his own existence and experiences.

[31] Existentialism - the philosophy that truth can only be established on the basis of one's personal experiences. Truth and meaning in life are completely subjective, and thus relative, differing for each person. Existentialism spawned the phrase, "You have your truth, and I have mine."

Euthanasia or Suicide

The idea that suffering people would be "better off dead" is usually based on one of two faulty assumptions: 1) all people go to a place of comfort, rest, and bliss after they die, or 2) there is nothing after death. Thus, either way, it is assumed if people kill themselves or others help them die, they will be in a better state than they are now in their suffering.

Those who assume all people go to a place of peace and rest when they die usually do so because they have been influenced by the Christian doctrines of heaven and hell. Rejecting the Christian teaching on morality, they incorrectly assume the "hell" portion of the teaching must be false. Certainly no one could be bad enough to go to hell, could he? God would not allow anyone to go to a place of eternal torment, would He? Reasoning thus, they assume the only place people can go when they die is to heaven, or an equivalent environment.[32]

The problem with this assumption is if the concepts of heaven and hell are revealed in a body of texts originating in the mind of God, then the Bible is true, and both places are real. Rejecting the notion of hell is then only a personal preference, unrelated to the truth revealed in God's Word.

If the Scriptures are a true revelation from the mind of God, and a person dies, he will either go to heaven or hell. And if the person is not a believer, then he will not be better off dead, but rather in a place of eternal torment. In that case, it would be better for the person to live as long as possible, regardless of the temporal suffering, so he can have a chance to turn to God, and escape eternal punishment.

The second assumption, that there is nothing after death, is usually based on a naturalistic, atheistic, evolutionary view of man. Since man is only an accident, evolved by chance through natural causes, then when he dies, there is nothing in man that persists after death. The brain produces the mind, and when the brain dies, the personality simply ceases to exist.

---

[32] This is sometimes attended by the silly, unbiblical notion that people become angels when they die.

The logical problem with this position is it cannot be proven. Based on the questionable notion of evolution, there is no empirical evidence available to prove there is no afterlife. Since there are competing philosophies of death, like Christianity, which claim to have information from an infinite mind about these matters, the person who asserts there is no afterlife does so in the face of evidence to the contrary. What if he is wrong, and the Scriptures really are the Word of God? Since there can be no empirical proof for his position, he cannot be sure a suffering person will really be better off dead.

Hinduism

Hinduism has two major answers for the question of suffering—maya and karma.

Maya (illusion) makes questions about suffering meaningless, because it claims all of reality is an illusion, including all suffering and pleasure. If what we experience as reality is actually only an emanation of an infinite, impersonal force of some kind, then it cannot be "real" in the sense we normally use that word. Hindus sometimes liken the world to the dance of a dreamer, where the dreamer is "god" and the dance is the world. One day the dreamer (god) will awaken, they say, and the dance (reality) will simply disappear. Thus, to them, the world is no more real than a dream.

Karma, a kind of moral cause-and-effect principle, answers the question of the innocent suffering by denying there are any innocent parties. If a person is suffering, then he must have done something in this life, or a former life, to deserve the pain he is now experiencing. Suffering is individual and personal, equivalent to the evil committed by the person prior to that time.

Though this idea may appear similar to the Christian teaching that the world is corrupted because of the sin of the human race, it is different in one crucial way. In the biblical worldview, people can suffer as innocent parties because of the choices of other people. In Hindu philosophy, every person is responsible for his own actions, and suffers for only those actions.

It is not too difficult to see how the idea of karma can cause great confusion when it comes to individual responsibility. For example, if one person injures another person, then karma says the person being harmed was supposed to be harmed because that is his karma returning to him. But where does that leave the person who is committing the harm? Is his action going to produce good or bad karma for him later in this life or a subsequent life? His choice was the vehicle for the other person to receive the bad karma he deserved. So was the choice good or evil?

When it is applied practically, the idea of karma actually produces more suffering in a society. If a person helps another person by relieving his pain, he may be helping him avoid the karma he deserves, thereby committing an evil deed himself. If people are consistent with the doctrine of karma, they will not help others who are suffering, lest they produce bad karma for themselves. Thus, suffering increases in any society where karma influences people not to help alleviate the pain of others.

Maya and karma may be consistent with the basic assumptions of Hinduism, but they are inconsistent with each other. If everything is an illusion, then pain and pleasure are both illusions, so which is better? Not only that, but karma itself is an illusion. So if good karma and bad karma are both illusions, which illusion is better?

Maya and karma try to answer the question of the innocent suffering, but fail to provide a solution because either 1) there are no innocent parties (karma), or 2) suffering and pleasure are both illusions (maya), and there is no basis to choose one illusion over the other.

Buddhism

People often forget the Buddha was a Hindu, so they do not keep in mind Buddhism is really reformed Hinduism. Thus, the answers of maya and karma for the problem of suffering will also be part of any Buddhist answer for the existence of evil. And as in Hinduism, maya and karma fail to answer the question of suffering from the Buddhist perspective as well.

But the Buddha did reform Hinduism, and so some of the tenets of Buddhism provide additional answers to the problem of evil beyond the basic Hindu elements. The four noble truths[33] (teachings about suffering), the fourth of which leads to the eight-fold path[34] (a basic set of moral obligations), are offered to help mitigate or eliminate suffering in a person's life. For our purposes it is not necessary to elaborate the details of Buddhism here. The basic idea is that suffering comes from desire (attachment), and to eliminate suffering you must eliminate desire. The way to eliminate desire is to observe the eight-fold path, which is basically a set of behavioral imperatives similar to the intuited moral codes of most other religions, including Christianity.[35]

Buddhism comes close to the Christian answer for the problem of evil by suggesting suffering comes from evil human choices. The Buddhist starting point is slightly off, though, and so the end result is very different from the Christian answer. Buddhism posits that suffering comes from *desire itself*, and so strives to eliminate desire. Christianity suggests suffering comes from evil choices, or from the *misuse of desire*. So while biblical teaching urges the correct use of desire, Buddhism requires the elimination of desire itself. The Buddhist follower must become completely impersonal, having no ambitions or desire, and ultimately become one in essence with the infinite, impersonal force that is the source of all things. Thus, to alleviate suffering in the world, or at least in one's own life, the Buddhist must become something other than a human being (i.e., enter Nirvana, or nothingness). Needless to say, no Buddhist is capable of fully living the philosophy of Buddhism. The desire to have no ambitions is itself an ambition.

It might be good to note here neither Hinduism nor Buddhism offers any answers as to whether or not evil is infinite or finite. Buddhism, at least, suggests a finite source of evil, since it comes from the desire of finite beings. Even the Buddhist suggestion that evil is somehow part of all matter will not answer the question,

---

[33] Life means suffering. The origin of suffering is attachment. The cessation of suffering is attainable. The path to the cessation of suffering. (See http://www.thebigview.com/buddhism/fourtruths.html)
[34] Right View, Intention, Speech, Action, Livelihood, Effort, Mindfulness, and Concentration. (See http://www.thebigview.com/buddhism/eightfoldpath.html)
[35] There is a superb illustration of why all religions produce similar moral codes in "Illustrations of the *Tao*," an appendix of C. S. Lewis's book, *The Abolition of Man* (New York: The MacMillan Company, 1969).

because matter is still only part of the illusion of existence. Still, both philosophies address the current problem without attempting any answers for some of the ultimate questions about suffering.

Mysticism

Pretending suffering has some intrinsic value is yet another inadequate answer for the problem of evil. Both Christians and unbelievers fall prey to this kind of reasoning, but from different perspectives, and with different results.

Unbelievers often adapt the "It's all good" or the "What doesn't kill you makes you stronger" attitude toward suffering. When they do this, they are assuming suffering has some kind of intrinsic ability to produce positive results in the lives of those going through painful experiences.

But if this were true, then all people coming out of a hospital should be better off psychologically than when they went in. Reality does not support this theory, though, as many people who experience the same trauma have very different reactions to their pain. Some do respond with greater strength, courage, and endurance after their ordeals, but others fall into depression, anger, or withdrawal from social relationships, and some commit suicide as a result. If all suffering produced better people, then we should not see these negative reactions. It is easy enough to deduce that the suffering does not produce the outcome, but rather it is the person's reaction to the suffering that generates positive or negative results.

Many Christians also adopt this faulty reasoning, only with a more spiritual slant. They sincerely believe God causes people to suffer so some kind of good can result in the person's life. This confusion results from a failure to keep two things separate—the suffering itself, and God's redemptive actions in the midst of suffering. People often remark, "Look at all the good things that have resulted in my life because of my experience." Then, instead of thanking God for helping them in spite of the situation, they mistakenly respond, "God must have wanted me to go through this suffering. Thank you God, that I was (born deformed, paralyzed in a car accident, shot with a gun, got cancer, etc.)."

God's redemptive actions in the midst of suffering do not mean the suffering was something God caused, or ever wanted to happen. It simply means God is good to us in spite of the fallen state of the world. God created the world as "very good," and we caused its corruption by our rebellion against our Creator. He never wanted us to experience all the pain and agony we see in the world, and it is still His will that no one suffer. But He must deal with the world as it is now, and that means helping us in the midst of our self-inflicted troubles.

One of the verses distorted by a mystical view of suffering is Romans 8:28.[36] Though it is commonly quoted from the KJV as "all things work together for good," the Greek grammar indicates a better rendering would be "God works all things for good." So it is not the "things" that work in our lives, but rather, it is God Who working in the midst of all the things in our lives. He can bring good out of any bad circumstance.[37]

It is also good to keep in mind that Romans 8:28 states there are conditions for God's actions in a person's life—they must be those who are called by God (Christians), and they must love Him (make the proper response to Him). Thus, this promise does not apply to the lives of unbelievers. In those cases where God works in the circumstances in an unbeliever's life, it is because of His mercy, and the response God is attempting to elicit is repentance.[38]

Yet another way some Christians view suffering as mystical or mysterious is to suppose everything that happens in the universe is the will of God. Some theologies actually teach that every event, and every choice, whether good or bad, is somehow God's will, and He has a purpose for every tragedy. There are two ways one

---

[36] Which I have affectionately nicknamed "the Christian fatalist verse."

[37] While the Greek manuscript $\mathfrak{P}^{46}$ adds the words "o θεος" to the text so the subject will be clear, these extra words are not necessary to establish that it is not the "all things" doing the work. There is an excellent article by Tim Geddert on why the grammar supports "God" as the subject, even without the extra words. You can find that article at:
http://www.mbseminary.edu/files/download/geddert1.htm?file_id=12815136.

[38] Romans 2:4 "Or do you think lightly of the riches of His kindness and forbearance and patience, not knowing that the kindness of God leads you to repentance?"

can view the world, given the condition that everything is God's will.

First, you could say God controls every event, and directly makes both the good and evil happen. This would be the absolute predestination of all events.

Second, you could conjecture the world is somehow going to involve both good and evil, and though God does not make it happen directly, still it will occur exactly as He has seen it in His foreknowledge.

Either way, when a person comes to the crucial point of making a choice, he will make the choice he does, either because God makes him do it, or because that was the way it was going to be from all eternity anyway.[39] In either case, the person may think he has true freedom, but because it was determined beforehand what he would choose, he really does not have a free will.

Now some readers may think this is a description of very rare and extreme cases, but this theology is taught in more churches than one would think.

For example, a missionary I worked with was in his home church in the US when he heard this startling comment from the pulpit. His pastor started a sermon with a statement like, "Now if I were to tell you every child who is born deformed, every war that is waged, every woman who is raped, and every person who is murdered, is all the will of God, that would be really hard to swallow, wouldn't it?"

My friend, who was in the congregation, thought, "Yes, and I wouldn't believe it, either."

But the pastor continued with, "Well, it's the truth, so you may as well get used to it." He then proceeded to teach that every event in human history is the will of God, because it was all planned by God before anything was created.

---

[39] This view of history puts God in the strange position of contemplating a series of events that will inevitably happen, but events that are not of His making. So who created the history of the world? If it was not God, then who or what? If history originated from a source other than God, then are we worshipping the true God, or should we be looking elsewhere? Absolute predestination makes more sense than this, but either view eliminates free will.

My missionary friend managed to endure the sermon, supposing such teaching was well over the heads of the congregation, and in the end, people would not live practically according to such a doctrine. But he found out later, in his counseling of the young people, that the people really were listening carefully. When he confronted a young man about his lifestyle of fornication, urging him to repent, the young man responded with, "Well, since everything I do, whether good or bad, is all the will of God, why should I stop?"

Even if one supposes every evil thing God plans for the universe ends up in some kind of good, you would still have a situation where God is doing evil that good may come. Romans 3:8 tells us we are forbidden to do evil (lie) so good (the promotion of the Gospel) may come. The Scriptures declare very boldly that if we do this, our damnation is just. And yet people assume God can do evil that good may come, and somehow that is different. But if God forbids us from doing this, why should He be exempt? If we are commanded to live in love, as He lives in love, then what is evil for us should be evil for Him as well. Does God make people suffer so He can work out some kind of good in their lives? He certainly does not.

John 9 and the Man Born Blind

One passage of Scripture gives many readers the impression God sometimes causes people to suffer so He can display His glory. The story, found in John chapter 9, seems to imply God made a man blind so He could manifest His works in the man by healing him.

This text bothered me for many years until I read the passage straight through in the Greek. I was reading this passage because of its reference to the word "sin," but as I did, I saw something I had never seen before.

The early Greek manuscripts were written in all capital letters, most had no punctuation except paragraph breaks, and there were no spaces between the words. So John chapter nine, verses three and four might have looked something like this:[40]

ΑΠΕΚΡΙΘΗΙΗϹΟΥϹΟΥΤΕΟΥΤΟϹΗΜΑΡΤΕ
ΝΟΥΤΕΟΙΓΟΝΕΙϹΑΥΤΟΥΑΛΛΙΝΑΦΑΝΕ
ΡΩΘΗΤΑΕΡΓΑΤΟΥΘΕΟΥΕΝΑΥΤΩΗΜΑ
ϹΑΕΙΕΡΓΑΖΕϹΘΑΙΤΑΕΡΓΑΤΟΥΠΕΜΨΑ
ΝΤΟϹΜΕΕΩϹΗΜΕΡΑΕϹΤΙΝΕΡΧΕΤΑΙΝΥ
ΞΟΤΕΟΥΔΕΙϹΔΥΝΑΤΑΙΕΡΓΑΖΕϹΘΑΙ

Because of the way the text was written, spaces between words, accents, breathing marks, and punctuation must be supplied by the translators. Most often these additions are helpful, but there are instances where the translation is influenced by the theological presuppositions of the translators.

As Roger Forster commented about this passage, it is most often translated the way it is because of "convention and prejudice"—"convention" because it has always been translated that way, and "prejudice" because the translators really believe God made the person blind so He could heal him. Roger also noted these translations represent God as completely different in character from the way He is described in the rest of the Scriptures. If these translations are accurate, this would be the only place is the Bible God is described as doing something evil to an innocent person so good could result.[41]

The wording of most English versions gives the idea God made the man blind so He could display His glory in the man. But that would be doing evil so good may result. This is how the text is translated in the New American Standard Bible:

---

[40] I say "something like this" because many of the manuscripts abbreviated words related to God, the "sacred names" or *nomina sacra*, and many other words in order to save space. In this sample the words are all spelled out fully.

[41] Roger made these comments over breakfast while visiting my wife and me at our mission base in the Netherlands. That would have been sometime in the 1970's.

Jesus answered, "*It was* neither *that* this man sinned, nor his parents; but *it was* in order that the works of God might be displayed in him. We must work the works of Him who sent Me as long as it is day; night is coming when no man can work."

In the Greek, however, the words "it was," "that," and "it was" are simply not there. That is why they are in italics in the NASB. If you read the text as the Greek reads, without the additional English words, you see the question is answered first, and then Jesus goes on with His original business of healing the man.

Jesus answered, "Neither this man sinned, nor his parents. But in order that the works of God might be displayed in him, we must work the works of Him who sent Me as long as it is day; night is coming when no one can work."

In other words, "Enough of these questions about whose fault this is. We need to be getting on with the work of the Father." Thus, with different punctuation, and without the extra words from the translators, the meaning of the passage is very different. The disciples were discussing why the man was born blind. Was it because he sinned (maybe in a former life?), or that his parents sinned? Jesus' answer was simple and straightforward—it was neither. So, in essence, Jesus did not really answer the question. Then, turning to the most important issue, He carried on with the work of His Father to heal the man.

Is Evil Necessary?

In the past few years, I have heard a number of people present a mystical view of evil that concerns me greatly. It is the view that evil is not actually evil, but really is good. Somehow, they say, the evil we see in the universe is happening for the ultimate good of the universe. If the evil were not there, then the universe would not be the "best of all possible worlds" God could have created. Or perhaps the universe will not be "optimal" if evil is not a part of the history. This is not a new idea, of course, but it causes me great concern that truly intelligent and godly people entertain and propagate this concept of evil. The question, of course, is whether or not this view of evil is true.

As a teacher, there are different ways I test what I believe, and what others say, to determine whether or not I accept the idea as true. The most important test, of course, is whether or not the idea can be supported by the Word of God, the Bible. But there are other ways, too.

Another major test is whether or not the idea aligns correctly with the eternal nature and character of God, and finite reality as God created it. As part of this second test, I like to compare "truth claims" with the major events in history, to see if the claim would be true at any time, past, present, and future. If a teaching cannot be reconciled with the following events, then its truthfulness should be questioned:

- **the nature and character of God in eternity past** (before the creation of anything finite, and before the existence of evil)
- **the act of creation** (including spiritual beings, and the first act of rebellion by Lucifer)
- **the creation of man** (made in the image of God, and possessing free will)
- **the rebellion of man** (the entrance of sin into the world)
- **the plan of redemption** (basically, biblical history from man's rebellion to the birth of Jesus)
- **the life of Christ** (including His birth, life, death, burial, resurrection, and ascension)
- **the second coming of Christ** (including the resurrection of the dead)
- **the judgment of all finite beings** (some to eternal joy, and some to eternal torment)
- **the new heavens and earth** (wherein dwells only righteousness)
- **the state of God and man in eternity future**

When I was attending Bible college, I saw this principle applied in class by one of my fellow students. In a course on practical Christian living, the teacher presented the idea that any time we are tempted, it is because we have somehow violated one of the principles from God's Word. This sounded plausible, until one of the students in the back of the class raised his hand, and asked, "So which principle from God's Word did Jesus violate, that He was tempted in all points, just as we are?" The teacher had no answer. The student had compared the teacher's idea with the life of Christ, and the principle did not withstand the scrutiny of reality. Needless to say, the class was over for the day. To her credit, the teacher changed her mind about the erroneous notion, shared her change of mind with the class, and removed the teaching from her curriculum.

Many aspects of the topic of suffering require close scrutiny through comparison with reality. One idea is the notion God arranged for evil to exist in order to produce a "greater good" in the universe. One aspect of this argument for the necessity of evil is the development of positive character qualities in the face of evil.

Gregory Koukl, a Christian apologist, put it this way in one of his articles:[42]

> For example, certain virtues couldn't exist without evil: courage, mercy, forgiveness, patience, the giving of comfort, heroism, perseverance, faithfulness, self-control, long-suffering, submission and obedience, to name a few. These are not virtues in the abstract, but elements of character that can only be had by moral souls. Just as evil is a result of acts of will, so is virtue. Acts of moral choice accomplish both.[43]

---

[42] Please keep in mind in the following arguments, that I am not attacking Gregory Koukl as a person, but simply disagreeing with some of his ideas. I greatly respect the work Mr. Koukl is doing for God and His kingdom. I am not "picking on" Mr. Koukl by quoting him. Rather, I am paying him a compliment, since his article is well written, making it easier to address than the rambling, narrative style of some authors. He will most likely disagree with many of my ideas, too, so if we can enter into lively, friendly discussion, I would welcome it.
[43] *Augustine on Evil*, Gregory Koukl:
http://www.str.org/site/News2?page=NewsArticle&id=5124.

But none of these "virtues" would have been necessary if Adam and Eve had not sinned.[44] Nor will they be necessary in heaven. They are only useful in light of the fallenness of the world. If the world were unfallen, how many people would need to be forgiven (if no one sinned), how many would need to be comforted (if no one were ever hurt), how many would need courage (if there were nothing to make them afraid)? A person's courage in the face of fear is admirable here, but will be completely useless in heaven, where there will be nothing to fear. A person expresses courage here in order to help others, which is praiseworthy, but in heaven that need will never exist. We may give comfort to those suffering here, but in heaven, where no one is suffering, that "virtue" will be completely useless.

Thus, if we examine the idea that it is necessary for evil to exist so certain character qualities could be developed, we see these qualities are only necessary in light of a fallen world. Compare this teaching with the whole history of reality, and we understand this philosophy of the necessary existence of evil is deeply flawed.

Again, the idea that God helps those in a fallen world by bringing good moral qualities out of a horrible situation is very different from saying God arranged the horrible event so the quality could be developed. Bringing good out of a bad situation produced by someone else is very different from producing the bad situation yourself.[45]

Another thing to keep in mind is that those character qualities we deem "virtues" are not developed *because of evil*, but rather *in spite of evil*. It is a person's proper response to evil that develops these character qualities. If the presence of evil in the universe developed these virtues automatically, then we should all have

---

[44] There is a mixture of different "virtues" listed here, some of which are necessary in light of the fallenness of the world, such as courage, and some that would be required of all beings at all times, such as obedience. My explanation should make it clear I am discussing the former.

[45] At this point people usually become inconsistent, claiming that people bring about evil by their choices, but God never intended that it exist. If this is so, then God could not guarantee that the "greater good" or "plenitude" of the universe would exist, since He could not guarantee that people would choose to do evil. So evil had to be part of the will and plan of God for the universe before He ever created. He had to guarantee that evil would exist.

these qualities in our lives. But people have to choose to be courageous in the face of fear. Some people do not make this choice, and so do not develop a courageous character. If a person does not choose to empathize with those who are suffering, then that person may remain bitter and resentful concerning his own suffering.

Evil, on its own, does not produce virtues. Our *proper response to evil* develops those character qualities. Koukl clearly states these character qualities are developed by choice, in response to evil. The problem is he then goes on to assume because God helped a person develop a virtue in the face of evil, then God must have arranged for evil to exist. But there is another problem with this position. If virtues are the results of human choices, then God could have never guaranteed any virtue would ever exist as a response to God's necessarily evil universe.

Lest someone think I am just picking on one item out of Koukl's argument, here are some quotes showing the context of his assertion about the necessity of evil. Each quote is designated with a bullet (•) and followed by a response:

• They[46] miss the big picture, though: God would not have accomplished a second purpose. He not only wanted free creatures; He also wanted plenitude, that is, the greatest good possible.

This is pure speculation. There is no biblical basis for such an assertion.[47] As far as I know, the only biblical statement as to the motivation behind God's creative act is "for His glory."[48]

---

[46] "They" is referring here to the philosophers J. L. Mackie and Anthony Flew.

[47] Normally I would welcome philosophical speculation, but in this case, I need to see some biblical support for the argument. Since Koukl is going to go on to say that God wanted evil to exist so the "highest good" could result in the universe, then I think he should have some Scripture substantiating that point. Unfortunately, there is none.

[48] Isaiah 43:7. I suppose that inasmuch as "because of Thy will" could be translated "for Thy pleasure" in Revelation 4:11, that could be another reference supporting why God created all things.

Speculating that "plenitude" was part of the motive for God's creation amounts to eisegesis.[49]

- Plenitude--the highest good, the best of all possible worlds--requires more than just general freedom; it requires moral freedom, and that necessarily entails the possibility of evil.[50]

The *possibility* of evil is completely different from the *necessity* of evil, which is what Koukl, following Augustine, proposes. Still, if the "best of all possible worlds" is one where people have the *freedom* to choose good or evil, then God accomplished His purpose.

- Since all that God made is good, even those things which appear evil only appear that way because of a limited context or perspective.

So, if I just look at rape differently, it will look good? If the Bible does not call evil good, then how does a person gain the perspective necessary to see the evil in the universe as a good thing? And if it is not possible for human beings to have this perspective, how could anyone rise above the level of human being to know this perspective is possible? Claiming "all that God made is good" does not help, because Koukl also asserts though all

---

[49] The forcing of a pre-conceived idea onto the Scriptures.

[50] Koukl is responding here to the idea presented by Mackie and Flew that God could have created beings with a free will, but without the ability to make "moral" choices. But what choice is not moral? If some of our choices are not moral, then why is it we will give an account of "every act" "whether good or evil" (Ecclesiastes 12:14; 2 Corinthians 5:10)? God seems to think all of our choices are moral. They may not all have the same import, but they are all either good or evil. Even though I might not pay attention to it, my daily, seemingly non-moral choices are all related to my ultimate intention in life. I am either actively living for myself or for God, and all my choices flow out of that motivation. (Jesus described this as a good tree producing good fruit, or a bad tree producing bad fruit.) So whether I think about it or not, all of my choices have a moral quality.

things are good, *choices* can be evil. Then he claims "evil" is a thing when it fits with his presupposition.[51]

Practically speaking, what do I tell my fellow Christian missionary who was raped just outside the gate of our mission property in the Netherlands? Do I tell her God arranged this evil so she could learn something about Him? Or do I tell her in the long run she will realize going through this trauma was for the "greater good" of the universe? How do you think she would respond to that explanation? God has something to say to those who speak in this manner: "Woe to those who call evil good and good evil."

Note, too, the subtle implication in Koukl's statement that everything that happens in the universe is the will of God. Everything God made is good, he reasons, so if something looks evil, then your perspective must be limited, because it is good, despite its evil appearance. He must be referring to choices here, and not metaphysical entities, because in his article he supports Augustine's assertion that all "things" are good in themselves, and only choices can be evil.

- When viewed as a whole, that which appears to be evil ultimately contributes to the greater good. A world that had never been touched by evil would be a good place, but it wouldn't be the best place possible.

Where in the Scriptures is the evidence for this? To say God had to make the best of all possible worlds, or what the nature of that world would be, is complete philosophical speculation, and not a biblical definition of reality. God did not reveal to us what was in His mind before He created. We only know God made the world, not what kind of world He was trying to make.

We do know, though, God has commanded us to abstain from all evil. Does this mean if everyone were holy, then the world would be a lesser place? What about the world before Adam and

---

[51] This mixing of the categories of metaphysics and morals, quite common in Augustine's arguments, surfaces frequently in Koukl's article. If evil is not a thing, then one cannot claim it is good because God made all "things" good. One can only reach that conclusion if one has already assumed that evil is a "good" thing God created. This amounts to circular reasoning—a non-sequitur.

WHY DO THE INNOCENT SUFFER?

Eve sinned? God said it was "very good." Was the world a better place after their rebellion? What about heaven before Lucifer sinned? Was heaven not as good a place before Lucifer rebelled, and a better place afterward? What about heaven in the future? Will it need a little evil mixed in so it can experience the highest good?

- The best of all worlds would be a place where evil facilitated the development of virtues that are only able to exist where evil flourishes for a time.

Again, this is total speculation. If the best world results through the existence of evil, then why would God command Adam and Eve not to sin? And as stated already, the virtues developed in the face of evil will be useless in heaven. If the "greater good" consists of character qualities that only help during the existence of the fallen world, then does the universe return to a state of "lesser good" when there is a new heaven and earth with no circumstances in which these virtues will be useful?

If God produced the "best of all worlds" by assuring there would be evil in the universe, then He did evil so good might result. We are forbidden to engage in such behavior (Romans 3:8), so why do we think God would participate in an agenda where the end justifies the means?

- This would produce a world populated by souls that were refined by overcoming evil with good.

What about children who die before they are born (having done neither good nor evil, as Paul states)?[52] Are they somehow inferior to those adults who had to face evil in the fallen world?

- The evil is momentary. The good that results is eternal.

Try telling that to the people who will spend eternity in hell. Is that somehow for the "eternal good" of the universe? Why then does God say He has no pleasure in the death of the wicked, but

---

[52] Romans 9:11.

rather they would repent and live? Why does God want all people to be saved? Why does God tell us we should not sin? God seems to be trying to eradicate all evil. Isn't He then working contrary to the "greater good" of the universe He made?

When theologians appeal to a "secret will of God" where He decreed evil should exist, as opposed to the "revealed will of God" in the Bible that God is against all evil, we have to ask, "Where did the theologians find out about this secret will of God?" If it was not from the Bible, where God reveals He is against all evil, then they must have constructed this idea with their own minds.

Another Example

The notion that God somehow wants evil to exist to bring about the best possible universe is not the idea of just one theologian. Just to illustrate that point, here is another example.

Dr. William Lane Craig, a Christian theologian, said this about his February 1, 2013 debate with Dr. Alex Rosenberg, an atheist:

> "It's possible that only in a world that is suffused with natural and moral evil that the optimal number of people would come to know God freely, find salvation, and eternal life," he continued. "So, the atheist would have to prove that there is another possible world that has this much knowledge of God and His salvation in it, but which is produced with less evils (*sic*). How could He possibly prove that? It's pure conjecture. It's impossible to prove those things."[53]

Since the idea of an "optimal" world is similar here to the world of necessary evil Koukl imagines, I will only present

---

[53] This is a quote from: http://www.christianpost.com/news/atheist-says-hell-turn-christian-if-evil-is-explained-during-major-debate-89362/#VMqoAZLHyo8TMs9l.99 Please keep in mind that as with Gregory Koukl, I am not attacking Dr. Craig as a person. He is doing a great service to God and His kingdom through his work in apologetics. I simply disagree with his description of an "optimal" world as an explanation for the necessity of evil.

objections relevant to Dr. Craig's quote. They are not in any particular order.

Objection #1 - The idea of an "optimal" world is complete speculation, and cannot be supported by Scripture. The Scriptures tell us God created the world, and describes the nature of that world, but the Bible gives us no indication whether or not the world, as it now exists, is an "optimal" creation.

Objection #2 - This view assumes the only possible kinds of worlds God could create would all include evil in some form. According to this supposition, a world without "natural and moral evil" could never be "optimal," so any world God created would need to include some amount of evil. To put it another way, if a particular number of people need to "find salvation" for the world to be "optimal," then a particular number of people need to be lost, so a particular amount of evil must be committed. On the other hand, if no one ever committed evil, then the world could not be optimal, because no one would need to be saved.

Objection #3 - On a sliding scale going from complete good to complete evil, God would have had to determine the exact amount of evil that would produce the "optimal" results. This means the history of the world was determined before it was created, and thus free will is eliminated. All choices in the history of that world had to occur exactly as God had determined, or God could not guarantee the results would be optimal. This means for any choice made in that history, it had to occur in a particular manner, and that means the person was not free to choose one way or the other.[54] The phrase "come to know God freely" does not

---

[54] For example, if one saved person in this "optimal" world was going to be a person born illegitimately, then the parents had to commit fornication or adultery when faced with the temptation. They could not choose otherwise, or the person would not be conceived, and the world would not have the "optimal" number of saved people. Claiming their choices were both determined and free

make any sense in a world that must contain a certain amount of evil to be "optimal."

Objection #4 - Can we ask why only some people being saved is "optimal"? Why is it God reveals He wants everyone to be saved, but thinks privately it is better that certain people go to hell? How does God determine an "optimal" number of saved people, if that is not every person? To put it another way, what would God consider the "optimal" number of people in hell?

Objection #5 - This idea of the world assumes God has absolute control over whether or not evil is committed, thus making God the author of evil. If an "optimal" number of people must be saved, then they cannot be saved "freely." Any argument that choices can be both determined and free is just so much logical and verbal nonsense.

Objection #6 - This notion assumes God's will is always done in every situation. This is contrary to the Bible's clear teaching that God's will is not always done.[55]

Objection #7 - As with Koukl's idea of the necessity of evil, God did evil that good may come.[56] He had to

---

at the same time is the same kind of nonsense as saying God can create "square circles" or "four-legged tripods."

[55] Chapter 4 of my book *Why Pray?* gives the biblical evidence for this point.

[56] Lest anyone should think I am unduly picking on the idea that an "optimal" world must include evil, listen to any of Dr. Craig's videos on evil, readily available on the internet, and you will see I am actually being conservative in my criticism. Most of his teaching starts with the idea that God had to make the world with evil included for the highest good of the universe to result. What? Does not the Bible say God created the world perfect? Was it not the sin of Adam and Eve that brought about the corruption of the earth? So God is good, and created the world perfect, and we destroyed it. And even before God created the world, was not heaven perfect before Lucifer sinned? This history does not lend itself to the idea that evil is necessary for the good of the universe. Only philosophical speculation about a hidden agenda that is contrary to the revelation of the Scriptures can support such a supposition. That speculation usually includes either 1) the idea that God predestined all events in the history

guarantee there would be a particular amount of evil in the world so the "optimal" number of people would believe. How can God unequivocally tell us evil should not happen, and we should abstain from all evil choices, when He knows an exact amount of evil must occur for the optimal number of people to be saved.

Dr. Craig claims the atheist will need to prove the "optimal" view of the world is false. But the atheist does not need to prove anything. Since it is the Christian who is supposing an imaginary world, the burden of proof is on him to produce some kind of evidence this is the way the world really is. The atheist has no obligation to disprove the philosophical speculations of the Christian by proposing some alternate kind of "optimal" world where there is less evil than our current creation. The real world, without the speculation, is already impossible for the atheist to explain, given his presuppositions.

This mystical view claiming evil is somehow actually good, or it is necessary in the universe, does not answer the basic question as to how evil originated, or why innocent people can suffer in a world created and governed by a benevolent God. This kind of speculation is counterproductive and unnecessary. The Bible already gives a sufficient explanation why evil is in the world, and why God, in most cases, cannot morally stop it, or its consequences, from happening.

The Example of the Godhead

If the universe needs to include suffering for the "best of all possible worlds" to result, or if evil is necessary for the "optimal" number of people to be saved, or if people must face evil in order for certain positive character qualities to be developed, then it seems one would have to question why God the Father, God the

---

of the universe, or 2) the idea that God's absolute foreknowledge of the future means the future objectively exists, and must transpire as He has already seen it. Either way, there is no free will, for man must inevitably live out the history God has either already planned or foreseen.

Son, and God the Holy Spirit seem so intent on preventing any evil from existing.

The Lord commanded Adam and Eve not to sin by eating of the tree of the knowledge of good and evil. He communicated to them the dire punishment and consequences that would result should they choose to rebel. If He secretly wanted evil to exist, then why go to such lengths to keep them from sinning? Once they did sin, He moved in history to bring about the salvation of the world through His Son. All along He appeared to hate evil, and encouraged the people He created to adopt the same attitude. The Bible tells us nothing of some hidden agenda that the evil in the world is somehow for the good of the universe. It only portrays God as working to encourage righteousness, and when evil did occur, He did what He could to mitigate the effects of man's rebellion.

When Jesus came, He seemed determined to stop evil in any way He could. He taught people to follow the law of God and be as loving and holy as possible. Not only did He work to encourage people to obey God, but He also labored to remove the consequences of evil whenever He could. He healed the sick, raised the dead, forgave the repentant, comforted the brokenhearted, and eventually died so all people could be saved from sin. Are these the actions of someone who secretly knew evil had to exist for the "optimal" outcome of the world to result?

God the Holy Spirit also seems determined to work against evil. Jesus said He would come to sort the wheat from the chaff in people's lives so the chaff could be removed. He convicts the world of sin, righteousness, and judgment, and that is to the believer's advantage.[57] He helps us put to death the deeds of the body.[58] Do these sound like the work of a Being who believes it is somehow better for evil to exist?

Though the workings of evil and suffering may be a "mystery" in some senses, there is absolutely no mystery when it comes to the attitude of the Godhead toward sin. They are unequivocally and adamantly opposed to any evil or its consequences. So the idea that evil is somehow a part of the great plan of God to make the

---

[57] John 16:7-11.
[58] Romans 8:12, 13.

universe a better place is simply an unbiblical and illogical construction of the finite mind of man.

Chapter 3

The Biblical Answer

The Bible gives us all the information we need to formulate a satisfying answer to the problem of suffering. Unfortunately, some philosophical and theological presuppositions in the church obscure the truth, keeping many believers from adopting the simple, obvious explanation for the corrupt condition of the world, and its continuation in that state.

There is a fear in the Body of Christ today, one that keeps people from believing or speaking the straightforward, clear teaching of the Bible on the topic of suffering. What is this fear? It is the fear of free will. Believers are actually afraid to stress the importance of man's freedom for fear of diminishing the greatness and glory of God.[59] This fear results from theological assumptions such as the idea that God has predestined every event in the history of the universe, or everything that happens is the will of God. People seem to reason if man truly makes free choices that are not controlled by God, then man would somehow be greater than God, thus attacking God's transcendence. But this reasoning is very flawed, and here is an example to illustrate that point.

Some artisans in the Muslim world have a curious custom. They deliberately make a mistake in their creations—rugs, pottery, jewelry, etc.—because they want to demonstrate only Allah is perfect. The problem with this reasoning is they assume if they were not to add the defect, then the article would have been perfect, thus contradicting their premise. They display by their

---

[59] Or fear that someone else will accuse them of denigrating God's glory.

actions that they believe they can make perfect works of art, if they should so choose.

Many Christians participate in this same faulty reasoning when they deal with the free will of man. They do not want to denigrate the glory of God by emphasizing man's freedom. But God has already made man with a free will, and man's creation was for the glory of God.[60] Thus, by thinking they must de-emphasize finite moral freedom in order to magnify God's greatness, they reveal their belief in the extreme value and impact of man's free will.

Once, during my missionary service, I was approached by a young man who had obviously heard something about my teaching.

"I hear you don't believe in the sinful nature of man," he said, a slight note of defiance in his voice.

"Well then, you heard wrong," I replied. "I believe in the sinful nature of man. I just don't believe in an inherited nature, passed down from Adam, that causes all men to sin. I believe man develops a sinful nature by his rebellion against the law of God."

"So then you believe man can save himself," he said. His logical "leap" quite surprised me.

"Do you believe because I don't accept the commonly taught idea of an inherited sinful nature, that I therefore believe I can offer an atonement sufficient for my sin, forgive myself, cleanse myself from all sin, and give myself eternal life?"

"Well, I guess not," he admitted.

"Neither do I," I responded. We then went on to have a lengthy conversation about the nature of sin. When we finished, he admitted our thinking was really very similar on the topic, and he should not have supposed to understand my ideas without talking with me.

People make these same kinds of logical "leaps" with the free will of man. But emphasizing the significance of human free will cannot diminish the glory of God. Rather, it enhances God's glory, power, and intelligence by declaring He could create beings in His image, deal with the risks such freedom entails, and accomplish His purposes in spite of any choices human beings or other moral beings might make. Working together with billions of free moral

---

[60] Isaiah 43:7.

agents to accomplish His will shows far more intelligence and creativity than forcing those beings to do what He wants. It is also far more interesting than thinking God is sitting in heaven, watching the same re-run of history for the millionth time, knowing all along how the story will end.

The answer to the question of the innocent suffering lies in man's freedom of choice. If we are brave enough to speak God's truth from His Word, we can explain the presence of evil in the universe, and offer the church and the world a biblical, intellectually-satisfying answer to the problem of pain.

Background Information - How Reality Works

In order to understand the origin of evil and suffering, it is first necessary to explore how God made the human race, and the environment he created for them to inhabit. Understanding man's essential nature, and the nature of those things that are "not man," helps people comprehend the situation both mankind and God must deal with when making choices relative to their environment.[61]

One might be tempted to assume God's Word does not really say much about the relationship of man to his surroundings, but that assumption would be a mistake. The Scriptures tell us far more than most people think, though the information must sometimes be inferred from the text, since it is often more implicit than explicit. Here is an example.

When I teach on apologetics, I like to point out that the humanist, with only his own finite mind, cannot establish the absolutes necessary to conclude the things around him absolutely and objectively exist. They might just be projections of his consciousness (if *that* really exists), and not real at all. He has no way to prove his surroundings exist apart from his experience of them. And then he must be continually skeptical of his experiences.

---

[61] I first heard this description of reality from a teacher in the Youth With A Mission School of Evangelism in Lausanne, Switzerland. I later learned these ideas are actually gleaned from Chapter 2 of *The Problem of Pain*, by C. S. Lewis (The Macmillan Company: New York, 1962).

I then ask the class whether or not the Bible tells us if the things around us are real. It usually takes a few tries, but the students eventually think of the book of Genesis and the creation. After a few hints, and a little help, some have actually come up with the answer. And just how does finite man know the things around him objectively exist apart from his experience of them? Because the Bible reveals man was created on the sixth day.

It is true some students are still scratching their heads at this point, wondering what I might mean by that. The Bible is a revelation from the infinite mind of God, and God, who was also an eyewitness of the creation, has revealed to us that finite objects, such as trees, animals, earth, seas, stars, etc. existed objectively before the finite mind of man ever existed. Thus, we have verification from an infinite mind that our finite experience of external objects as real is accurate and can be trusted.

This kind of information, more implicit than explicit, is found throughout the Bible. We just have to read carefully and apply our minds to God's Word to discover these implicit truths. It is the same with God's creation of man in His image. There are many things we can glean from the Scriptures, if we are willing to do the study and exert the thought necessary to find them.[62]

God created man in His image and likeness. This means God made human beings to have intellect, emotions, and will—the basic elements of personality—so they could contemplate, make decisions, and then enjoy the consequences of those choices.[63]

---

[62] Bernard Ramm calls this the hermeneutical principle of inference. Simply stated, it goes like this: that which can be logically inferred from a text applies with as much force as the actual statements of the text. *Protestant Biblical Interpretation* (Grand Rapids: Baker Book House, 1970), pp. 128-148.

[63] I cannot take the time or space here to back up every statement, but there are good, biblical reasons for my claims. For example, God said, "If any man draws back, *my soul* has no pleasure in him." So God is a Spirit (John 4:24) who has a soul (Hebrews 10:38). In the Bible, the capacities of intellect, emotions, and will are ascribed to the soul. (See Appendix A of my book, *Understanding the Cross*, for a list of references.) This is also how we generally define the personality of man. Thus, God, who has a soul (personality), created man in His image to also have those same capacities of personality. This is how man is in the likeness and image of God.

In order to make man in His image, God also had to make man self-aware.[64] As part of this self-awareness, man had to know who he was, and that there was something else—the "other" that is around man, or his objective environment. This was necessary because a being must be aware of himself, and what is not "himself," before he can make reasonable, deliberate decisions relative to his environment.[65] To put it another way, self-awareness is necessary if a being is going to have a free will.

Something else that is necessary for free will to exist is alternate choice. If the power to choose exists, but there is only one end that can be chosen, then one could argue the ability to "choose" does not exist, since the definition of "choose" includes a difference between at least two ends. Maybe one could define this as the power to "act," but it could not be actual choice. To choose always implies alternative ends, so free will requires alternatives.[66]

---

[64] With reference to God's self awareness, it is interesting, and almost comical, how God tells the people of Israel that He knows of no other God besides Himself, and then asks them if they can find one like Him. (Isaiah 44:6-8 ; 45:5, 6) This proves He is obviously self-aware, and also knows that there is no other being like Him.

[65] Again, it is not obvious, but the Scripture passages about the unity and diversity in the being of God (i.e., the trinity) support the idea that God has both subjective and objective aspects to His being. Thus, just as we exist in an objective environment, so the members of the Godhead also exist objectively to each other. It has always encouraged me to know that when God communicates moral law to us, He has both subjective and objective proof that the law He is requiring of us is absolutely the correct way for man to live. And He does that with infinite understanding.

[66] Oddly, there are some theologies that teach man is free to choose, but he can only choose to do evil. People who hold this position want to have it both ways. They want to say that man is free, and thus responsible for his choices, but that the only act man can make with his will is to do evil. The fallacy here should be obvious. The word "choose" is being defined as having alternatives when they speak of the responsibility of man, but the same word is defined as having no alternative when they speak of man's actual actions. This is called equivocation, or changing the definitions of your words at different points in your argument. (But then, is not a person who acts, even if every act is evil, making a choice between the alternatives of action and inaction?) For our purposes, though, we will use the word "choose" to imply that alternative choice actually exists, since that is the way it is used in the Scriptures. See Deuteronomy 30:15-19, Joshua 24:15, 2 Samuel 24:12, Proverbs 1:29, Isaiah 7:15-16, Philippians 1:22.

Once self-awareness, free will, and alternatives exist, then responsibility is inevitable. If moral agents are free to choose between alternatives, then the consequences in the external environment (the "other") will either be for the good of the object, or for its detriment. To put it another way, when a person is faced with choosing for the well-being or the ill-being of another person, then he is responsible to select one alternative over the other. This constitutes the basic understanding of "right" and "wrong."[67]

Now we come to the crucial point for our questions about suffering. The only way a person can know what will result when he makes a choice is if the environment in which he exists is stable. If the environment were changing all the time, he would not know which of his choices would be beneficial to others, and which might be destructive. If medications could change their effect at any time, a doctor would never know if his prescriptions were going to help or harm the patient. He would not be able to choose a treatment if he could not depend on the result in the person's body. If food could change its chemical structure to become poisonous at any time, it would never be safe for a person to eat. So the environment into which agents make choices must be stable.

Further, in order for the environment to be stable, it must be governed by laws that are an intrinsic part of the objects themselves. An object that could be changed by the subjective whim of a person would never be trustworthy to another agent in that environment. Unless the object itself is subject to laws that make it maintain its properties, then alternative choice would be impossible, since the results could not be predicted accurately.

Next, if God creates beings in his own image, who must live in a stable environment governed by laws, then the environment cannot change to accommodate the wishes of different beings. What is agreeable to one person may not be agreeable to the next. My wife and I face this problem constantly. When the room is warm enough for me, it is too cold for my wife. When the

---

[67] Jesus used this same argument, based on the value of the object, to establish that "it is **lawful** to **do good** on the Sabbath." Jesus taught that moral responsibility is derived from the perception to choose one end over another— the well being of a man over that of a sheep.

temperature is warm enough for my wife, it is too warm for me. Amazingly, the air does not change its temperature to accommodate the wishes of the person it touches.

To use another example, if one person is walking down a hill, then a person walking in the opposite direction must walk up the hill. The hill does not change its physical properties to accommodate the desires of the different walkers.

Lastly, if a stable, predictable environment is necessary for free will to exist, then the environment can be used in different ways by different people. This is an old example, but I find it very useful. If two people were in a cold room, and had some logs at their disposal, they could use the wood to make a fire to stay warm, or they could use the wood to beat each other unconscious, or even kill each other. The wood, however, is not going to change its properties just because someone decides to use it to perpetrate an evil act. Thus, the same stable environment that is necessary for the well-being of its inhabitants can also produce suffering, depending on the choices made by those living in that reality.

Therefore, when God made the world, He made it for our good, suitable to our needs as beings made in His image. But the same environment that is good for our freedom can also be used for evil, with the result that suffering can result from the same environment. To look at it from a different perspective, if we ask God to change what He created, in order to make it impossible for people to suffer, then we are also asking Him to take away our freedom of choice. But to take away our free will would be to make us something less than human, less than the image of God. Thus, He must leave the environment as it is, even if we cause suffering through our misuse of what He has created.

The Origin of Evil in the Universe

According to the Bible, evil and its consequences had a finite beginning in the universe. Isaiah 28 gives the story of two beings related to the city of Tyre. Verses 1-10 describe the "leader" of Tyre, evidently the human leader of the city, while verses 11-19 describe another being, the "King" of Tyre. Though it is possible these descriptions could be of the same person, it is more likely a description of two different beings, distinguished by their qualities.

The first being is described as a man, apparently uncircumcised, whose wisdom is compared to that of Daniel. This leader used his wisdom to acquire gold and silver, until his heart was "lifted up" and he actually thought of himself as a god. He was able to be attacked with swords, wounded, slain by a ruthless nation, and then go down to the pit (Sheol). All of these qualities indicate this being was human—the physical leader of the city of Tyre.

On the other hand, the "King" of Tyre is attributed very different qualities. He had the "seal of perfection," full of wisdom, and perfect in beauty. He was in Eden, which could not be said of the human leader of Tyre, and his covering was precious stones. God apparently gifted him with musical talent, as the workmanship of his tambourines and flutes was in him on the day he was *created* (unlike the leader of Tyre, who had to be born as a man). God then calls him a cherub, a particular species of spiritual being. Some have two wings, and some have four, but they all have four faces on one head (man, eagle, ox, lion), two hands, one body, and two feet. Unlike the leader of Tyre, who took power to himself by his wisdom, the "King" of Tyre was placed as an anointed leader by God Himself on the "holy mountain of God." His job was evidently to "cover" or "protect." He was blameless (infrequently said of humans) until he sinned ("unrighteousness was found in you"). Therefore, God cast him out from the "mountain of God," from the "midst of the stones of fire." The "covering cherub" became proud, and his wisdom was corrupted by reason of his splendor.

Though some of these qualities could be applied metaphorically to a human leader of Tyre, some are simply beyond the scope of the normal human being. It seems more likely this is a description of the spiritual power, or principality, "behind" the human leader of the city. If so, it fits well with other descriptions of Lucifer (Light Bearer), or Satan (the adversary), the "serpent of old," who is also called the devil (liar).

We also know this being made his choice to rebel against the law of God before he tempted Eve in the Garden of Eden.

Precisely how long before that time Satan sinned is not recorded in the Scriptures. It would appear, though, since Satan was cast out to the earth,[68] that his rebellion happened after the creation of the world, but before his tempting Eve in the garden. Regardless of when it happened, though, Lucifer was the first to commit an evil act, creating evil in the universe for the first time.

Paul the Apostle tells us in Romans 5:12 it was through Adam that sin entered into the world. So, just as Lucifer introduced evil into heaven, so Adam introduced evil into the earth. In both cases, evil was "created" by the finite choices of a moral being.

Unfortunately, evil choices do not affect only the beings who make them. The consequences of rebellious acts all too often affect other innocent beings. As a result of Adam and Eve's choice to rebel against God, God was required, by His love and justice, to judge them and the earth. From another passage in Romans, it appears as if Adam's choices affected not just the earth, but the entire creation.[69]

Thus, evil consists of the choices of finite beings, and the consequences resulting from those choices. Evil is finite, and it appears to have affected the entire finite, created order.

Why God "Allows" Suffering

Two inevitable questions come to mind if God created a finite world, and then some of those creatures rebelled, bringing about the existence of evil, and the resultant consequences.

First, why would God allow this to happen? Why couldn't He just stop evil from happening in the first place? A person's view of God's relationship to moral law is going to play a big part in how he answers this question.

Second, now that evil exists in the universe, why doesn't God do something to protect us from it? This question is phrased in various ways, but some common examples could be, "Why did this baby have to be born deformed? Why didn't You stop the car accident from happening? Why did my brother have to be hit in the

---

[68] Revelation 12:9.
[69] Romans 8:19-22.

drive-by shooting? Couldn't You have done something to stop these tragedies from happening?"

These questions appear at first glance to deal mostly with the free will of man, but they really concern God's response to man's free choices. It is a matter of perspective. It is not that man limits God by His choices (though it could be spoken of in those terms), but rather God limits His own choices so as not to negate man's freedom and significance.

There are two ways to define the word "allow." The first way is to say "allow" means God is free to stop all evil choices, and the attending consequences, but for some reason unknown to us, He simply chooses not to do so. This can leave us questioning the love, goodness, and justice of God. If He could stop someone from suffering, then why does He not intervene? In these cases, one would have to simply accept the "mystery," and trust God, even though it appears to be His fault the person is suffering. But since the Bible declares God is "just in all His ways, and kind in all his deeds,"[70] this definition of "allow" is inconsistent with the revealed character of God.

An illustration might help here. If there were two people in wheelchairs, and one fell to the floor by accident, and the other threw himself to the floor, whose fault is it that they are on the floor? Well, for one person it was an accident, so you could blame the general fallenness of the world for that person's plight. But for the one who threw himself down, you would have to say it is his fault. Now, let's consider the caregiver who is responsible for both people. If he picks up the one who fell by accident, but leaves the other man on the floor, whose fault is it one person is in his chair, and the other is not? Even though the person who is on the floor is there by his own choice, we must still blame the caregiver for the disabled person's continued stay on the floor, since the caregiver could have helped him up also.

In the same way, if we brought about the destruction of the world by our sin, but God could have stopped all the negative consequences to our choices, then it is His fault the world continues in its fallen state. It makes no difference if the suffering

---

[70] Psalm 145:17.

in our lives is our fault or someone else's, it would still be God's fault it does not stop.

But there is another way to define the word "allow," one taking the will of man, the will of God, and the significance of the human race into consideration in the definition. It involves only a slight change in perspective, but it requires a complete change in the definition of God's character. If "allow" is defined as "God can do whatever He wants, and whatever He does is right," then God can be completely arbitrary when it comes to moral law, and no one can question His actions or motives. However, if we define "allow" to mean "God must respect the freedom of choice of a moral being, even if the consequences are severe," then for God to "allow" evil and suffering takes on a completely different definition. It also frames God in a completely different light relative to moral law. Using this second definition, God is not free, in most cases, to interfere with the choices of moral beings, but must allow them their freedom, even if it means innocent parties might suffer as a consequence.

For some people, this view of God's relationship to moral law, namely that He must submit to the law of love, is a very threatening concept. They think God should be able to do whatever He wants, whenever He wants, and no one should be able to question His actions. But that is not how the Scriptures present God. Throughout the Bible we see Him reasoning with people, and even being challenged as far as His justice is concerned, and yet He does not tell the person asking to keep quiet. With regard to the destruction of Sodom and Gomorrah, Abraham said, "Shall not the Judge of all the earth deal justly?" The Lord did not tell Abraham not to ask, or fault him for questioning His justice in the case. Instead, God reasoned with Abraham, listened to his prayers, and granted him his request.[71]

One particularly revealing illustration of God's limitation when dealing with people is found in the book of Isaiah 5:1-7. There God uses a metaphor, in the form of a song, likening Himself to a vinedresser, and the nation of Israel to His vineyard. Just as the vinedresser does everything He can to make the vineyard produce

---

[71] Please see Chapter 1, footnote 16 for an explanation of how Abraham's request was granted by God.

good grapes, so God does everything He can to encourage Israel to do righteousness rather than evil. Then God makes this amazing statement. "What more was there to do for My vineyard that I have not done in it?" In other words, "I did everything I could, but they still chose to do evil." What a statement! God, the Creator of all things, the Lord of the universe, infinite in wisdom and power, *did everything He could*, but it was still not enough. The idea that God will not force people to do what is right is not just the construct or desire of some finite human mind—it is the clear teaching of the Scriptures. Sometimes everything God can do is not enough, because He so respects the free will of man.

If God is going to be just, following His own law of love, then He must "allow" people their freedom. This entails two parts, the choices themselves, and the consequences of the choices. To curtail their choices would not only deny them their freedom as beings made in the image of God, but would also remove the significance of their choices, and thus their significance as humans. On the other hand, removing the consequences of their choices would have the same effect. Since the consequence of a choice is what makes it significant, then to remove the consequences of a choice makes the choice itself meaningless.[72]

So, except in rare cases, God must "allow" people their freedom of will. To put it another way, He *cannot justly stop* the free-will choices of moral beings, and He *cannot suspend the consequences* of their choices. To do so would remove their significance, and make them something other than beings created in God's image. This is not a matter of power. Obviously God has all the power He needs to keep any finite moral being from making a choice. Rather, it is a matter of God's submission to His own moral law which makes it unjust to interfere in the freedom of the creatures He made. It is a moral restriction He brought on Himself by creating finite beings who also have the power of free will. In this way, God *must* "allow" suffering, even the suffering of the innocent.[73]

---

[72] Obviously, I take a telic, rather than deontological view of morality. I give my reasons for this position in Chapter 1 of my book, *Why Pray?*
[73] There is more about God's relationship to His own law in Chapter 5.

Another word that can be used with two very different meanings is the word "cannot." This word can be used to indicate metaphysical impossibility ("I cannot touch my elbow to my ear"), or it can be used to indicate a moral impossibility ("I cannot murder my wife"). They can even be used in the same sentence, with different meanings, and still be clearly understood. If I ask the owner of my local convenience store if he can sell me his store for one dollar, he might say something like, "Yes, I can. But no, I cannot." Even though he said both, I understand what he means, because he is using the same word in two different ways. "I can" means he is capable of receiving the dollar, and changing the title of the franchise to belong to me. "I cannot" means the store is his livelihood, and for his and his family's sake, he cannot sell me the store. The first "can" is metaphysical, the second "cannot" is moral.

The Bible uses the word "cannot" in reference to God when it says "God, who cannot lie." Though most people do not think much about this, they can understand what is being communicated by "cannot." This does not mean God is incapable of saying, "Two plus two equals five." Rather, it means because of God's commitment to love and holiness, He is morally incapable of communicating something untrue to another being. Thus, if God "cannot" lie, then the statement "God cannot stop most evil" is perfectly reasonable within the biblical framework of God's character. He is physically able to stop evil, but His commitment to justice and holiness will not allow Him to interfere unjustly in the choices of other moral agents.

Probably the simplest example of this principle is the salvation of a human being. God wants all people to be saved, and is actively working to influence them in that direction. But if a person refuses to repent, then God must "allow" him to continue in his sin. He cannot justly force the person to repent, so He must allow him to rebel, even if that means He must allow him to go to hell for eternity. To put it another way, hell shows the significance of man's free will.

So defining the word "allow" as "cannot justly stop" helps us understand many of the actions (or inaction) of God in situations of evil and suffering.

Does this mean God can never interfere with the choices of moral beings? No, in many cases He can, but in order to do so, He must have good moral grounds for His actions. In cases of influence, there is never a problem. God is free to influence any being, because His influence still leaves the person free to choose. But if God wants to do something that counteracts a free-will decision, He must have sufficient moral grounds. These grounds most often come in the form of agency from the same or another moral being. That agency can consist of prayer, obedience, praise, spiritual warfare, or a number of other activities, but it is always the result of the choices of some finite moral being.

Miscellaneous Points About Pain

What is Pain?

The physical or emotional experiences of human beings can be very hard, if not impossible, to define with words. This is especially true of an experience so basic as pain. Every person experiences it, but finding adequate vocabulary to explain it is a daunting endeavor.

Dictionaries are extremely unhelpful with subjects such as pain. The definitions go in circles, each defining itself using the vocabulary of another definition, one equally as puzzling as the next. Most definitions are explanations of what pain is not, and so avoid the problem of a positive description. Simply put, pain is extremely hard to define.

It is therefore both sad and fortunate that an accurate definition is not really necessary. Since every person experiences pain in some form (the sad part), we all know what someone means when they report they are in pain (the fortunate part). This is similar to the pleasurable experience of eating an orange. If a person has eaten one, then he knows what another person means when he says, "It tastes like an orange." But without the prior experience of tasting an orange, a person would be lost trying to understand a verbal description of the flavor.

Pain is difficult to define, but we have to start somewhere. After browsing many dictionaries, I was able to boil down the essential meaning of the word "pain" to this rather vague definition:

Pain - Any lack of comfort, being ill at ease physically, emotionally, mentally, or socially

The idea of spiritual pain did not appear in any of the dictionaries, but since a relationship with God is a personal matter, spiritual pain could fall under the category of social pain.

It's All a Matter of Degrees

One of the interesting things about pain is that the same stimulus that produces pleasure can also produce pain. It all depends on the degree of the stimulus. A person can place his cold hands close to a fire, and experience a pleasurable warmth. If he puts his hands too close to the fire, he can experience the pain of burning. The stimulus—warmth—is the same in both cases. It is the degree of the stimulus that produces either pleasure or pain. Another example would be putting pressure on a person's body. Done in one manner, often called a massage, there are pleasant sensations. But if a person pushes hard enough on another person to dislocate his shoulder, then suffering results. It is all a matter of the degree of stimulus.

The reason the difference between pleasure and pain depends on the degree of the stimulus is that the same bodies that can experience pleasure can also experience pain. This presents the interesting question as to whether or not God could have created us to experience pleasure, but not at the same time have the capacity to experience pain. Medical research will probably have to answer that question. But He did create us to experience both, and that may have been as a safeguard for us should we choose to sin. He knew the possibility of man's rebellion against His loving government, and thought of a plan of salvation before He even created man. Following the same reasoning, maybe He created us with the possibility of pain for our protection, should we decide to reject Him, and live for ourselves.

The New Jerusalem, situated in a new heaven and a new earth, is going to be a place where there is no pain.[74] This statement could mean one of two things. Either resurrected human bodies will not have the capacity to feel pain, or there may be nothing there to produce any pain. Either way, we will have to wait to know for sure. The wonderful news remains the same, though—one day, pain will be no more.

Pain Can Be Useful

Not everything about pain is bad. Dr. Paul Brand and Philip Yancey wrote a book called *Pain: The Gift Nobody Wants*.[75] Why did they refer to pain as a gift? Because it is a warning device, signaling us when something is wrong with our bodies. Without pain, we could bleed to death internally, and never know it was happening, or at least, not know until it was too late to save our lives.

Consider the plight of people who have advanced leprosy. The disease can cause them to lose feeling in their bodies due to damaged nerve endings. In some poor countries, people with leprosy are sometimes bitten by rats at night, but have no pain reaction to awaken them. This can result in the loss of fingers or toes to the rodents, or to subsequent infections. Leprosy patients can also experience damage to their feet because they do not feel the need to change their gait while walking. Fortunately, special shoes have been developed to protect their feet. These same shoes are helpful for diabetes patients, who sometimes lose feeling in their extremities because of their condition.

As useful as pain is, however, it is only necessary for our well-being in light of the fallenness of the world. Once we are in a perfect place, where there is nothing that will harm us, we will no longer need pain to alert us to danger. Thus, while pain is very useful to us now, it is only because of the fallen state of the world. One day pain will be abolished.

---

[74] Revelation 21:4.
[75] Diane Publishing: Darby, PA, 1999.

Pain and Selfishness

Pain can act as an influence on our actions. The contemplation of pain can encourage us to avoid choices that might result in pain. Take, for example, the drug addict who overdoses, but does not die. That person will often think of the possibility of that kind of pain before he uses drugs again. In that way, just the thought of pain encourages abstinence, even if those choices might be ultimately self-serving.

God uses the consequence of pain as an influence towards obedience. Any quick review of a list of punishments for disobedience will reveal how often God mentions pain as a deterrent. For example, the familiar list of punishments in Deuteronomy 28 includes:
- consumption
- fever
- inflammation with fiery heat
- being struck by the sword
- boils
- tumors
- scabs
- itch
- hunger
- thirst
- nakedness
- miserable and chronic sicknesses
- the diseases of Egypt
- sickness

Beyond all the temporal physical pain God uses to influence us towards obedience, there is the prospect of separation from God in eternal torment for refusing to yield to Him as Lord. "The wages of sin is death."[76] Of course, He warns us of these consequences in an attempt to keep us from experiencing them. His commands are always for our good,[77] and never meant to be a burden. He knows,

---

[76] Romans 6:23.
[77] See Deuteronomy 4:40 ; 5:16 ; 5:33 ; 6:3 ; 6:18 ; 10:13 ; 12:28 ; Jeremiah 7:23 ; 38:20 ; 42:6.

however, that we sometimes respond more quickly to the prospect of pain, than to the gentle admonitions of our Heavenly Father.[78]

---

[78] Though it is often said that Jesus spoke more of hell than He did of heaven, I could not verify this in my reading of the New Testament. Still, Jesus did speak frequently about hell, clearly indicating He was not against using the thought of eternal torment to influence people towards good behavior. These references reflect the subjects of heaven and hell in Jesus' teaching, and not just the words. The word "heaven" in the phrase "the kingdom of heaven" is only listed when it refers to an actual place. Please see:

Heaven (46) - Matthew 5:12, 6:20, 8:11, 10:23, 13:43, 16:19, 18:10, 18:18, 21:25, 22:30, 25:46, 26:64, 28:18 ; Mark 9:43, 45, 47, 10:30, 11:30, 12:25, 14:62 ; Luke 10:18, 20, 21, 11:13, 15:18, 16:9, 16:22, 23, 25, 26, 18:13, 18:30, 20:3, 20:35 ; John 6:32, 33, 38, 41, 42, 50, 51, 58 ; John 14:2, 3 ; Revelation 2:7 (?), 3:12.

Hell (38) - Matthew 5:22, 5:30, 7:19 with 7:23, 8:12, 10:15, 10:28, 11:22, 11:23, 11:24, 13:30, 13:42, 13:50, 16:18, 18:8, 18:9, 18:34, 35, 23:15, 23:33, 24:51, 25:30, 25:46 ; Mark 3:28, 29, 9:43, 45, 47, 48 ; Luke 1:12, 14, 15, 12:5, 16:23, 24, 25, 26, 28 ; Revelation 1:18.

Chapter 4

Varieties of Suffering

People tend to lump all suffering into one category in their minds. When they do this, they make it difficult to discover and understand the source of specific cases of suffering. Although all pain and suffering comes directly or indirectly from one general source—the evil choices of finite moral beings—there are still different ways these choices produce the consequences we see in the world. Understanding how the source of the suffering relates to the suffering itself can help people comprehend how God is not at fault in the suffering of the innocent.

When investigating the source of suffering, a helpful general principal to follow is "time and space." The farther apart the source of the suffering and the suffering itself are in time (chronologically) and space (geographically), the harder it is to discover the exact source of the suffering.

Take, for example, the two very different cases of a person who is shot during a mugging on the street, and a baby who is born deformed. Because the suffering and its source are very close in time and space with the shooting, it is easy enough to see why the person is suffering. The victim can readily understand he is wounded because of the malicious intent of another human being. Thus, it is easy to see God is not at fault in this case. But if a baby is born deformed, the cause for that deformity may be easy to discover, (e.g., the mother took thalidomide while she was pregnant), or it may be difficult because it is has various causes spanning multiple continents (space), and reaching all the way back to the fall and the flood (time). It may actually be impossible to pinpoint specific events that could have affected the genetics of the baby. It may only be possible to posit general causes for the deformity.

There is yet another problem people can have if they imagine all suffering as being in the same category. To many people, suffering is a very mysterious, vague, basically unknown quantity in their thinking. Unfortunately, God sometimes falls into this same category in their thoughts. He is mysterious, vague, and unknown. Thus it is possible to associate suffering with God in their minds, when there may be no connection between the two in reality. They then blame God for the suffering, when He had nothing to do with the events. As a result, the bitterness and resentment they feel about the suffering can be projected onto God, causing conscious or unconscious strain in their relationship with Him.

The Malicious Intent of Other People

As far as the innocent suffering, probably the easiest cause to understand is when one person deliberately hurts another. This is because the cause of the suffering and the suffering itself are so close to each other in space and time. The cause and the effect are obvious, thus making the relationship between the two apparent.

This cause of suffering is also easier to divorce from God in our thinking. We know the perpetrator is responsible for the suffering, so we understand readily it is not God's fault. The cause is concrete, and not vague or unknown, so it is easily separated in our minds from the concept of God.

Still, some people may ask why God did not stop the person from harming someone else. The answer to this is obvious, though, as God cannot morally stop most choices, whether good or evil. He must respect the free wills He Himself created. He cannot just interfere in the decisions of moral beings without doing great harm to their freedom. And if He curtails their freedom, He removes their significance as beings. Thus, God is restricted from intervening, not because we can stop him by our choices, but because He respects the freedom and significance He instilled in us as beings made in His image.

On a more practical note, this source of suffering is often the reason for many childhood hurts, some of which continue to plague people into their adulthood. Whether by malicious intent, or by ignorance, adults often harm children who are under their care. Sometimes the adults are not caregivers, but only have access to the child. Either way, the injured child can carry the memory of that hurt into adulthood, and along with it the resulting behaviorial difficulties.

The sources of these hurts are often forgotten, or buried in a person's memory. They can be forgotten if they happened so early in the child's life that the person cannot remember them as an adult. They can also be buried by the person's mind as the young mind strives to protect itself from the hurt.

Uncovering these sources can bring significant healing for the adult who was mistreated as a child. If nothing else, when the person recognizes other humans are the source of the pain, and not God, this can free the person to have an open relationship with the Father.

Persecution for God's Testimony

When Christians preach the Gospel, they might be persecuted by other people. This persecution sometimes includes physical attacks. If the Christian has done nothing to harm the unbeliever, then the believer is suffering as an innocent party for the sake of the Gospel. Jesus warned us this would happen, so it should come as no surprise to those involved in evangelism.

But there are two ways a person can suffer for the sake of the Gospel—as an innocent party, or as a guilty party. As Peter tells us in I Peter 2:20:

> For what credit is there if, when you sin and are harshly treated, you endure it with patience? But if when you do what is right and suffer *for it* you patiently endure it, this *finds* favor with God.

Being persecuted for one's own sake may happen more than people realize. When I was working as a missionary on a military

71

base in Germany, a brother came to me, almost boasting he had been assaulted for the sake of Christ. Knowing this brother's propensity for rudeness in his speech, I asked him to recount the incident. After he told me what he had said to the unbeliever, I remarked I probably would have punched him too, even as a Christian, if he had said something so rude to me. "What you really need to do is to go back and apologize to the man," I said. "You have no right to rejoice in your suffering for the Gospel. Your suffering was your own fault."

When the early apostles suffered for preaching the Gospel, they rejoiced they had been counted worthy to suffer shame for the name of Jesus. Acts 5:41 records:

> So they went on their way from the presence of the Council, rejoicing that they had been considered worthy to suffer shame for *His* name.

Though some people interpret this text to mean the Apostles *rejoiced that they suffered*, this is not what the Scriptures say. It states they rejoiced that they were *counted worthy to suffer* shame for His name. Their lives were so much like the life of the Lord Jesus, the unbelievers had the same reaction to them as they did to Jesus—they wanted to kill them. So they rejoiced that they were considered worthy to suffer, but they were not rejoicing over the suffering itself.

In cases like this, it is easy to see how the cause of the suffering is directly related to the event of suffering. In this way, it is similar to being shot during a mugging. Persecution over preaching the Gospel happens because of the malicious intent of other people. The cases are different, though, because a mugging can happen for no reason at all related to the victim, whereas persecution most often happens due to anger over the actions or words of the believer. Still, both are examples of the innocent suffering.

Disease and Deformity

When a person is suffering because of the malicious intent of another human being, the cause is easy to discern. But what about those cases where a person is suffering, and there is no immediate human choice to blame? Who is responsible for the baby who is born deformed, or a person's genetic predisposition to heart disease, or cancer?

In some cases we can point to bad health habits, but not in every case. Maybe a person has lung cancer because of smoking, but what about the baby who is born with only one hand? Again, we can sometimes attribute even those cases directly to choices, such as taking thalidomide during pregnancy, but not in every instance. There appears to be a general degeneration of the human body that often cannot be attributed directly to the choice of a human being. So where does this corruption originate?

Many Bible-believing Christians do not think concretely about the history of the earth revealed in the Scriptures, and how those events can affect our lives today. Three of the major, world-changing events recorded in the Bible are the rebellion of man, the cursing of the ground, and the flood of Noah. Each of these events has a dramatic effect on our daily lives, even thousands of years after the incidents.

When Adam and Eve rebelled against God by eating from the tree of the knowledge of good and evil, they were punished for their actions by being denied access to the tree of life. Evidently, even in their fallen state they could have lived forever if they had been allowed to partake of that tree. It appears as if the thought of this prospect was so horrible to God, He did not even finish His sentence about the possibility.

> Then the Lord God said, "Behold, the man has become like one of Us, knowing good and evil; and now, lest he stretch out his hand, and take also from the tree of life, and eat, and live forever"—[79]

---

[79] Genesis 3:22.

Instead of finishing His sentence, God acted, in His mercy, to exclude man from the tree of life so people could not live on forever in their selfishness. Imagine the evil a 4000-year-old wicked person could teach the upcoming generations. Through this punishment, evil was curtailed, but the effect of this exclusion has had repercussions down to the present day.

The bodies of Adam and Eve were probably perfect when they were created, but that is certainly not so for our bodies today. Being excluded from the right to eat of the tree of life has affected every human being since the rebellion of mankind. Our bodies are no longer protected and regenerated by the influence of the tree. It is difficult to pinpoint the exact causes of the degeneration, but we do know certain elements in the environment, such as pollution, and certain behaviors, such as incest, can cause problems in the physical bodies of subsequent generations.

Thus, when a baby is born deformed, and there does not seem to be any immediate cause for the child's condition, there are general causes in the history of mankind for such effects. The fallenness of the human body is a sufficient cause for these occurrences. We may not be able to isolate the exact cause of the suffering, but one thing we do know is this is not God's fault. He warned Adam and Eve not to sin. God never wanted any children to suffer in this way, and He still does not want this. But He must deal with the world in the condition it is now, a condition we brought on ourselves by our own choices, and He does what He is free morally to do about the situation.

A second source for degeneration in our bodies is God's curse on the ground. It is not clear exactly what the extent of damage was to the creation because of the curse. If what Paul says in Romans is any indication, though, it appears as if the whole creation was affected along with the earth.[80] If this is true, then our bodies, as part of the creation, have been affected along with the rest of the physical material in the universe. Even if Paul's reference to the whole creation was meant to indicate just the earth, our bodies are still included in the affected area.

It is important to keep in mind that God's motivation in cursing the ground was loving, merciful, and just. When people have an

---

[80] Romans 8:19-22.

abundance of spare time, they tend to use it for their own selfish purposes, that is, they sin. In His wisdom, God cursed the earth, making it difficult to get food to grow from the ground, thereby guaranteeing people would be kept busy trying to grow their daily food. This was compounded by the growth of briars and thorns, plants that had not existed before, or at least not in that same form. It is difficult to tell from the wording in Genesis if this was an intended part of the curse, or simply a consequence of cursing the ground. Either way, more briars and thorns meant more difficult farming, and less time for leisure and selfishness. There was also a limitation of edible plants, since every green plant could be eaten before the curse, but many green plants are now inedible or poisonous.

Also, as with the curse on the ground, He multiplied the conception of women. In that way, God keeps them busy, and curbs their selfishness, by having to care for a greater number of children.

Deformity and susceptibility to disease can be explained on the basis of the fall of man and the curse, but there is another ancient, world-wide event that effects our physical bodies today. The flood, with all its destruction to the earth, from the fountains of the great deep, to the floodgates of the heavens, provides multiple causes for the entrance of disease and deformity into the history of man's physical lineage. The damage inflicted on the earth by the flood was so severe as to prompt God to call it another curse.[81] There are a couple of results of the flood that have continuing effects on the earth's population, so it is good to keep them in mind when thinking about how our bodies can suffer, even when there is no direct human choice to which to tie the pain.

After the flood, the lifespan of people shortened with each generation. Whereas people were living 700, 800, or even 900 years before the flood, a few generations after the flood humans were living only a little over 100 years. In a period of approximately 320 years, the lifespans listed in the genealogy of Genesis 11 decreased as follows:

---

[81] Genesis 8:21.

Noah - 950
Shem - 600
Arpachshad - 438
Shelah - 433
Eber - 464
Peleg - 239
Reu - 237
Serug - 230
Nahor - 148
Terah - 205

The remainder of the book of Genesis records similar lifespans:

Abraham - 175
Isaac - 180
Jacob - 130+
Joseph - 110

What produced this dramatic change in the length of human life? Though some would like to attribute this shortening of lifespan to God's pronouncement, "nevertheless his days shall be one hundred and twenty years,"[82] this would be a misapplication of the text. God made that declaration before the flood, not about how long people would live, but concerning how long it would be until the flood came. It does not refer to the individual lifespan of humans.

But something about the flood caused a reduction in human longevity. Could it be a change in atmospheric pressure, dramatic temperature and climatic changes, loss of nutrients in food sources, or exposure to harmful radiation from space? Though the cause of this change is a matter of much debate, even between Christians, the point is, we have not seen the lifespan of humans *increase* dramatically since shortly after the flood. Whatever caused this decrease is either still in effect, or has caused a permanent state of damage affecting all mankind.

Our bodies are not in the same perfect state as Adam's body before he sinned, so we are subject to deformity and susceptible to

---

[82] Genesis 6:3.

disease all our lives. We suffer as innocent parties every day because of the choices people made in the past, and it is important to recognize these sources of damage so we do not mistakenly blame God for suffering that is not His fault.[83]

Natural Disasters

Earthquakes, hurricanes, tornadoes, tsunamis, lightning strikes—these natural disasters all cause people to question God's relationship to the suffering produced by these events. Does God cause these events? If He does not cause them, why does He not rescue more people from the disaster?[84] These questions, and many like them, appear on our TV and computer screens shortly after the event. Unfortunately, many well-meaning Christians try to offer solace by suggesting God knew what He was doing in causing the destruction.

But who says God was involved at all? Well-informed watchers may be able to dismiss the inference that God is guilty for the devastation, but most people will assume the Christian must be right, concluding God causes events killing thousands of innocent

---

[83] Some might like to argue that since Adam sinned, but it was God who excluded him from the tree of life, then it is God's fault that babies are born deformed. But this is fuzzy thinking about God, moral law, and punishment. God, as the Moral Governor of the universe, is responsible to seek our well-being by enforcing sanctions (both positive and negative) for the law. Sanctions directed to our minds are the only way God can justly influence us toward keeping the law of love. When He does enforce the law, He is not being arbitrary, but is giving us what we deserve as a result of our choices. Thus, exclusion from the tree of life, the curse on the ground, and the flood are not God's fault, they are ours. So the results in a baby's body, if that child is born deformed, are due, in large part, to choices people made before the flood, and God is not responsible for the damage. For a detailed discussion of God's role as Moral Governor, please see Chapter 4 of my book *Understanding the Cross* (Xulon Press: Maitland, FL, 2007).

[84] Actually, I think God does intervene in these events far more than we think. We do hear stories of possible supernatural protection after such tragedies, but these are often missed (or dismissed) by the media, and they are very hard to substantiate. Anyway, God, like all other heroic first responders, is not interested in taking credit for doing His job. And even if He were involved, it would be hard to prove His activities, since He and His angels are usually not visible during these events.

people. So why would God do this? "Well," says the Christian, "it's a mystery, and we just have to accept God's will."

"Hogwash" would be far too kind a word for this kind of answer. But before we examine some of the causes of natural disasters, let's take a look at the logic encouraging some Christians to offer this kind of response to these situations.

Why do insurance companies refer to natural disasters as "Acts of God"? Apart from the obvious motive of not wanting to pay the claims in these cases, they are employing the logical fallacy called "affirming the consequent." It goes something like this:

God is able to make earthquakes happen.
An earthquake happened.
Therefore, God made this earthquake happen.

This logical fallacy will be covered more fully in the next chapter, but for now, we can use this simple example to illustrate the bad logic:

If an animal is a cow, then that animal has four legs.
This animal has four legs.
Therefore, this animal is a cow.

In the same way a horse is an animal with four legs, but is not a cow, so an earthquake could happen, but have a cause other than God. An insurance company would call the tornado that killed Job's children an "act of God," but they would be wrong. Satan caused that tornado. That means there could be at least three sources for a tornado—God, Satan, or natural causes.

Just as deformity and susceptibility to disease are results of the choices people made before the time of Noah, so natural disasters would appear to have their origin in the same causes—the curse of the ground, and the flood. If the whole creation is groaning and travailing in pain until now, waiting to be freed from its corruption, then the earth could groan, and an earthquake happens. The earth could travail, and a tsunami could be born. Though God declared the earth to be "very good" when He created it, it is no longer in that condition. Our choices have brought about a devastation and corruption affecting the entire creation, and that corruption includes violent weather patterns, movements of tectonic plates, and many other possible causes of devastating natural events.

Before the flood of Noah, the circulatory system of water on the earth did not include precipitation in the form of rain. There were springs of water, and a mist went up from the ground to water the earth, but no rain. Then, when the flood came, rain became part of the water cycle in the earth.

So what would this have to do with the innocent suffering? If precipitation became part of the world because of the flood, then the choices people made before the flood are still influencing the earth today. God judged the earth back then, but the consequences of that judgment are part of our history in the present time. Any suffering related to precipitation is directly connected to pre-flood evil choices. To put it another way, if the deluge had not happened, no one would have ever perished in an avalanche of snow, or drowned in a flood, or starved because a hailstorm destroyed their crops. Between the rebellion of man and the flood, innocent parties could have suffered because of water, but not because of precipitation.

It is likely most natural disasters do not have supernatural sources, but are rather the result of natural causes. The only way we could know if the source of a disaster is supernatural would be a revelation from God. It is probably better to assume a natural disaster has a natural source, unless supernatural intervention is revealed as the cause. Speculation about the origin of such events may only cause greater emotional grief to those suffering because of the disaster.

Probability—Chance, Accidents

"Nothing happens to the Christian by chance!" "Everything happens for a reason." "There are no accidents in the life of the believer." Have you ever heard statements like these? It may seem reasonable, but the problem is, it simply is not true. It may sound comforting to think nothing accidental can affect the life of a believer, but would it really be wonderful if everything that happens in a person's life is either caused or permitted by God?

Apart from the Scriptural evidence that chance is part of our world, there are serious logical and practical problems one faces if chance never operates in the life of the Christian.

Perhaps an example will help illustrate this point. If a believer is walking by a building, and a loose brick falls at just the right time to hit him on the head, could this have happened by chance? Most people, including Christians, would look at this as a chance occurrence, that is, an occurrence that happened because of probability related to the cause-and-effect laws built into the universe. Other than the person's injury, most people would not assign any great cosmic significance to the brick's falling from the building.

But if there are no accidents in the life of a Christian, then the brick must have fallen because God caused it to fall, or because He could have stopped it, but did not. It is also possible some other finite agent might be responsible—perhaps an evil spiritual being. That seems to leave at least three possibilities. Accidents happen either:

1. Because of the cause-and-effect laws in the physical creation, or …

2. Because of the will of a finite moral being, either the person himself or another being, or …

3. Because of God's will. And that could be by *commission* (He caused it directly), or by *omission* (He chose not to prevent it).

Of course, only the first option actually describes events that happen by chance. If both chance *and* choice are involved in a seemingly accidental occurrence, then the "chance" part of it is not a relevant factor. If the brick could have fallen solely by chance, but it was actually an evil spiritual being who pushed it, then it was not really by chance. If God made the brick fall, or if He could have stopped it, but chose not to, then it was still not truly by chance. The brick fell because God wanted it to fall. Whether the choice is made by a finite being, or by God, the truly "chance" part of the event is eliminated.

Before investigating more closely whether or not accidents happen in the life of the believer, it might be good to look at a crucial aspect of the subject of probability itself. Since we have very little biblical information about accidents and probability, we must keep in mind much of this discussion will be based on speculation. We will look at some of the biblical evidence for chance and accidents a little later.

Because we can be hurt in accidents, we often assume any kind of chance is a terrible thing. But what if I drop a coin on the floor? It seems it really does not make much difference to my life whether the coin lands heads or tails up. Actually, it appears as if most of the chance occurrences in the world have no effect on humans, or at least have no detrimental effects. So probability is not evil in itself, though it can sometimes bring great harm to some people.

It is hard to imagine an early earth, prior to the fall, where nothing happened by chance. Could an apple bounce in different directions after falling from a tree? Would that mean future trees might grow in different places, depending on which way the apple rolled? What if a bee pollinated one flower rather than another, just because the wind happened to blow a different direction just then? Would the difference in pollination mean something was wrong with the number or kind of flowers that resulted? Rather, is it not possible that regardless of where the trees are, or which flowers grow, the will of God was accomplished in both cases because the plants were being fruitful and multiplying?

While it might be interesting to speculate whether or not Adam could have had a piece of fruit hit him on the head by accident, that is a moot point now, since the world is no longer in its perfect state. The world is corrupted, and so is the human race. The real question, then, is whether or not man's rebellion against God caused a change in the way the lives of human beings are impacted by the laws of the universe.

The logical possibilities related to chance occurrences before and after the fall are rather limited. These seem to be the more relevant possibilities related to chance, creation, and man:

1. The laws of probability and chance were the same before the fall as they are now. In other words, nothing changed relative to probability because of man's rebellion.

2. The laws of probability and chance were different before the fall than they are now. In other words, fundamental changes happened relative to probability because of man's rebellion against God.
3. Man is affected by chance the same way now as he was before the fall. In other words, there was no change in man, relative to chance, because of the fall.
4. Man is affected differently by chance now than he was before the fall. Or, man is affected differently by chance now because a change happened in man at the fall.

Certainly, these are not all of the logical possibilities, but they constitute a good starting point. We are told in the Scriptures both the creation and the body of man were corrupted at the time of the fall. What is not revealed is whether or not chance affects man differently now that these changes have taken place.

Since we know man's body was "very good" before the fall, and it is likely probability existed in the creation both before and after the fall, then we are prompted to ask, "What changed such that people could be hurt by accidents after the fall, whereas they might not have been affected before the fall?"

Proximity appears to be an essential element in whether or not someone is affected by an accident. It is not always the case, but a person is often not affected by an accident because he was not in the area when the accident happened. Take the "brick from the wall" accident suggested above. If the person is only a couple of feet in any direction from the path of the falling brick, then the person will probably not be affected adversely.

But what could make the difference between the same event before the fall, and after the rebellion of man? That difference could be knowledge. Because of unbroken fellowship and communication with God, humans may have always had instant knowledge of where they should be in order to avoid potentially dangerous accidents. Here is an example from my own life.

Once, when a brother and I were coming home from a night of sharing the Gospel, he stopped his car at a red light not far from our missionary home base. Because it was early in the morning, possibly 3:00 am, there were very few cars on the road. When the light turned green for us, and red for a car approaching from the right, I looked at the car, and "knew" the other car would not stop at the light. I said, "Stop. That car is not going to stop at the light." The brother stepped on the brake, causing the car to halt part-way into the intersection. Just then, when we would have been in the middle of the intersection, the other car ran the red light and sped through without even slowing down. If the driver had not stopped when he did, we would have certainly been hit by the other car. This is one incident that would have been considered a bad accident if God's supernatural knowledge had not been involved.

This kind of "divine protection" does not happen in every case, so how should we view those incidents where the accident does happen, and some people, even believers, are injured or killed? The answer here is the same as for the problem of unanswered prayer. It depends on whether or not God is morally free to intervene in our sphere of stewardship. God's freedom to intervene is based on the choices His stewards make in their area of dominion, that is, the earth. In the case of our being protected from a car accident, there were people from our mission who were praying for us that night. If someone prayed for us to be protected from an accident, it may have been enough for God to be free to protect us.

Of course, the questions really arise when someone is not protected. In those cases we must trust if God had been morally free to intervene, He would have done so. The complexity of the number of wills involved is staggering, and only God knows all of the factors involved in any one event. Therefore, in cases where God does not respond with protection, we must trust Him, and not accuse Him of some kind of indifference when we have no evidence to prove such motivations on His part. Here is another example illustrating we should not presume to know what God knows about a situation.

The founder of our mission once narrowly escaped a very serious car accident. He was thankful he was not involved, but could not point to any reason, other than chance, that he was not injured.

Later, in his travels in China, a woman he did not know approached him with a question. "On this day (she gave the date), were you almost involved in a car accident?"

"Yes," he replied. "That did happen on that day."

"God woke me up in the middle of the night and told me to pray for your protection."

When the founder realized her prayer would have been at exactly the same time as his possible accident, he then understood God had awakened the woman to pray for him. That way, God had a good enough moral reason to intervene in the man's life. Before he had this information, though, he did not know why he was spared in this possibly deadly event.

But some might wonder how important it is to pray, especially when some of His children pray for His protection, but are injured anyway. Since we can never be sure exactly which choices will free God morally to act, but He does know, then we do not know if our prayers will be the reason God is free to intervene. If we pray, and we are protected, then fine. If we pray, and we are not protected, we need to trust He would have helped if He had been free to do so. When He is free to act on our behalf is too complex for us to know. We simply need to pray, and trust Him to always do the just and loving thing in the circumstance.

Before moving on to what the Scriptures say about chance, let's take one more look at the logic behind the idea that there are no accidents in the life of the believer. It seems as if there are three possibilities that could produce a world where nothing happens by chance in a Christian's life. Those options include:

1. God controls every event in history so nothing happens that is not His will, or …

2. The history of the Christian is pre-determined so it cannot happen any way but what God wants, or …

3. God steps in actively to stop any event He does not want to happen in the life of a believer.

Though some people may find these ideas comforting, the end result is that any bad events in the life of a Christian are God's responsibility. It is His fault because He planned that it should happen (points 1 & 2), or it is His fault because He did not stop it from happening when He could have (point 3). If the only way to explain detrimental accidents in a person's life is to claim God caused or allowed it to happen, then these options may not be so comforting after all.

In spite of these explanations, some readers may still be questioning whether or not accidents can ever happen in the life of the believer. Well, no matter how interesting, or even accurate, our speculations about probability may be, the final authority on whether or not Christians experience chance occurrences will be the revelation of God's Word. Here are some verses to support the idea that chance is part of the world in which we live:

Ruth 2:3 - So she departed and went and gleaned in the field after the reapers; and she **happened** (Hebrew - chanced upon her chance) to come to the portion of the field belonging to Boaz, who was of the family of Elimelech.

I Samuel 6:9 - And watch, if it goes up by the way of its own territory to Beth-shemesh, then He has done us this great evil. But if not, then we shall know that it was not His hand that struck us; **it happened to us by chance**.

II Samuel 1:6 - And the young man who told him said, **By chance** I happened to be on Mount Gilboa, and behold, Saul was leaning on his spear. And behold, the chariots and the horsemen pursued him closely.

I Kings 22:34 - Now a certain man drew his bow **at random** and struck the king of Israel in a joint of the armor. So he said to the driver of his chariot, "Turn around, and take me out of the fight; for I am severely wounded." (II Chronicles 18:33)

Ecclesiastes 9:11 - I again saw under the sun that the race is not to the swift, and the battle is not to the warriors, and neither is bread to the wise, nor wealth to the discerning, nor favor to men of ability; for **time and chance overtake them all**.

Luke 10:31 - Jesus said - And **by chance** a certain priest was going down on that road, and when he saw him, he passed by on the other side. (Greek - κατὰ συγκυρίαν - and by a coincidence)

Acts 17:17 - So he was reasoning in the synagogue with the Jews and the God-fearing Gentiles, and in the market place every day with those who **happened** to be present. (Greek - those **chancing** to be there. Not the normal ἐγένετο, but παρατυγχάνοντας, from τυγχάνω - to come about by chance). Another verse using this same Greek word is I Corinthians 16:6, "and **perhaps** I shall stay with you." See also I Corinthians 14:10 ; 15:37.

While some of the above verses do not state directly that chance was involved in an incident rather than God, one thing those verses do tell us is the people involved in the events believed chance was a possibility in their lives. And while some people would like to say "at random" needs to be reinterpreted as "God did it," this is an imposition of an idea onto the Scriptures that could only be defined as eisegesis. Unless there are clear verses stating nothing happens by accident, then those texts affirming chance and accident in the universe should be interpreted as literal descriptions of the way the universe works. God knows better than we do how things work in His creation, so we should take His word on the subject as accurate and authoritative.

Attack of Spiritual Beings

People who dabble in the occult, or persist in rebellion against God, open themselves up to the attack of evil spiritual beings. Ephesians 2:2 describes Satan as "the spirit that is now working in the sons of disobedience." While people in this category might suffer under the attack of the enemy, they are actually guilty parties suffering for their own choices. On the other hand, there are cases of innocent parties who suffer under the onslaught of evil spiritual beings.

There are three major reasons wicked spirits attack innocent people. First, since they have their own will, they can attack human beings out of malicious intent, i.e., they do it just because they want to hurt someone. We see examples of this in the stories of demonized people in the New Testament, such as the little boy the demon tormented and tried to kill,[85] or the demoniac of the Gerasenes.[86] Second, they will sometimes attack people who are preaching the Gospel. Jesus was attacked in the wilderness, at the last supper, and on the cross. Satan resisted Paul in his efforts to spread the Gospel.[87] Third, evil spirits can attack people when God uses a righteous person's life as an example to the spirit as to how it should be living. This was the situation when Satan attacked Job. How this last attack works is explored in detail in the next chapter, but it will be good to preview the basics of this process here.

Apparently, God uses the lives of righteous people to teach His wisdom to spiritual beings. Ephesians 3:10 reveals this principle:

"...so that the manifold wisdom of God might now be made known through the church to the rulers and the authorities in the heavenly *places.*"

Note the wisdom of God is revealed to rulers and authorities in the heavenlies *through the church*. It appears the way this happens is God compares the life of a righteous person with the wicked lifestyle of a rebellious spirit. When He does this, it sets up a situation where God can be confronted with a moral dilemma. If the evil being questions the righteousness of the human, thereby also questioning how God is living, then God must allow a test of the person's life to proceed, if the wicked spiritual being insists. The test may not ensue in every case, but the possibility of attack is there due to the very nature of the situation. Also, this comparison may happen without God's deliberate intervention, since His wisdom can be revealed to the rulers and authorities just by the lifestyle of the believer.

---

[85] Matthew 17:14-18.
[86] Mark 5:1-20.
[87] I Thessalonians 2:18.

To put it another way, our choices have implications, even cosmic implications, and when God uses a righteous person's life to show a spiritual being how it should be living, then that being has a right, morally, to question the motives of the righteous example. Doing what is right without thought for any benefit—or disinterested benevolence—is how God lives, and how every other moral being ought to live. When God uses a righteous person's unselfish lifestyle as a moral plumb line against evil spiritual beings, they can respond by attacking the person God is holding up as a standard.

This, of course, is the whole story of the book of Job. The next chapter covers this principle in detail, so this should suffice to describe the process. Righteous people can suffer as innocent parties under the attack of evil spiritual beings just because they are living in disinterested benevolence.

Chapter 5

The Suffering of Job

There is one book of the Bible dedicated entirely to the subject of the innocent suffering—the book of Job.

Though the book explores only one reason for suffering, it does give us insight into many of the moral complexities of God's interactions with free-will beings. God's government over moral agents, God's commitment to living in love, the cosmic implications of our choices, dilemmas created by free moral agents, God's self-limitation in dealing with moral beings—all these and more are present in the short, 42-chapter text.

The book does not explain every reason for the suffering of innocent parties. Actually, compared to disease, deformity, natural disasters, and the malicious intent of other humans, it probably records one of the least frequent causes of suffering. Nevertheless, the principles revealed in the story are helpful in understanding other instances of the problem of pain and evil.

Exploring the book of Job is a rich and rewarding endeavor. Many people feel they just cannot understand the message of Job, or the actions of some of the characters, especially God. But through careful study and thought, the book can yield insights producing philosophical, theological, and practical benefits for the reader. The results of understanding the message of Job are well worth the effort.

Was Job Truly Innocent?

Many explanations of the book of Job start well, calling the text a case of the innocent suffering. But somewhere along the way, the writer assigns some kind of blame to Job—Job was fearful, Job was in unbelief, Job blamed God, Job was involved in some kind of secret sin he was unwilling to confess. Having begun well, the writer only becomes one more "miserable comforter,"[88] accusing Job of wrongdoing, but with no real explanation for Job's plight. So was Job truly an innocent person suffering?

The opinion of only one person is finally important in this regard—God. God said Job was an innocent person. Before the first test, the Lord tells Satan, "Have you considered My servant Job? For there is no one like him on the earth, a blameless and upright man, fearing God and turning away from evil."[89] After the first test, God repeated this description, and then added, "And he still holds fast his integrity."[90] Then after the second test, at the end of the book, God tells Job's comforters, "You have not spoken of Me what is right, as My servant Job has."[91] The Lord began by declaring Job blameless, upright, fearing God, and turning away from evil. God's final opinion of Job was that he spoke what is right about God. Since God never changed His estimation of Job's character, those who ultimately accuse Job of some kind of evil are incorrect. Otherwise, they portray God as either mistaken, at best, or lying, at worst.

Again, if Job had sinned, then why would Ezekiel hold him up as a standard of righteousness? He says of Job in Ezekiel 14:

"Even though these three men, Noah, Daniel and Job were in its midst, by their own righteousness they could only deliver themselves," declares the Lord God. (verse 14)

"Even though Noah, Daniel and Job were in its midst, as I live," declares the Lord God, "they could not deliver either

---

[88] Or "sorry comforter." Job 16:2.
[89] Job 1:8.
[90] Job 2:3.
[91] Job 42:8.

their son or their daughter. They would deliver only themselves by their righteousness." (verse 20)

Another evidence of Job's righteousness is presented in the book of James, when Job is held up as an example of a righteous person suffering under attack. Speaking of rich employers who are oppressing their workers, James describes their actions as, "You have condemned and put to death the *righteous* man; he does not resist you."[92] James then goes on to use the prophets and Job as examples of righteous people enduring suffering with patience:

As an example, brethren, of suffering and patience, take the prophets who spoke in the name of the Lord. Behold we count those blessed who endured. You have heard of the endurance of Job and have seen the outcome of the Lord's dealings, that the Lord is full of compassion and is merciful.[93]

It is interesting the only references to Job in the Bible, apart from the book of Job itself, are quotes reinforcing Job's righteousness. God, Ezekiel, and James all thought Job's character was exemplary. Thus, trying to imply Job sinned, especially during his trials, is in direct opposition to the testimony of the Scriptures.

The truly ironic thing about accusing Job of some kind of sin is that this eliminates the whole point of the book. If Job was guilty, and his comforters were correct, then Job was only suffering as a result of his own choices. Thus, to maintain the integrity of the book of Job as a treatise on the innocent suffering, we must agree with God, declaring Job blameless and upright through the entire story. It is the only way to make sense of the book.

God and Moral Law

For many people, the book of Job seems difficult to understand. But the basic themes of the book are easy enough to

---

[92] James 5:6.
[93] James 5:10, 11.

decipher. The difficulties arise when the reader's concept of God's character conflicts with His actions.

To many people, the idea that God had to allow Satan to attack Job simply does not line up with their understanding of God's relationship to moral law. In spite of the overwhelming evidence to the contrary in the Scriptures, people imagine God has no moral law to which He is responsible. They understand the law of love applies to them, but they seem unwilling to acknowledge it also applies to God. They somehow believe God is making up the moral law as He goes along, determining what is right and wrong by His own choices.

There are really only two ways to look at this—either God is not subject to any moral obligation, and whatever He does is right (by definition), or He has some kind of law He follows, and cannot do whatever He wants, but must do what is right according to that law. The question is, "Which of these describes how God lives?" And, if God has a law to which He must submit, where does God's moral obligation originate?

Jesus taught that moral law in the mind of humans is derived from the intuitive perception of the value of the object under consideration.[94] In other words, when we consider an object, such as a human being, we are intuitively impressed with the value of the being, and we perceive ourselves as obligated to choose "this" (well-being), and not "that" (ill-being) for the object. In this way, Jesus revealed the origin of moral law. It is "right" to do "good" based on the value of the object. How do we know it is more important to heal a man on the Sabbath than to rescue a sheep from a pit? Jesus says we know this on the basis of the difference of value between the man and the sheep.

This is probably a new concept for some people, so it is worth repeating. Moral beings perceive the value of objects under consideration, and are obligated to choose the well-being, rather than the ill-being, of that object. This is due to the inherent value of the object. And as the passage states, we also perceive the difference in value between objects, and are obligated to choose the well-being of the more valuable object over the one of lesser value. This does not mean the object of lesser value should be

---

[94] Matthew 12:9-14.

ignored, but simply, if there is a choice between the objects, we must choose for the more valuable object first.

For example, if my house is burning with my child inside, I know I should rescue the child first. But my house is also valuable, and if I can save it too, I should do so. I should just do it after I rescue my child. Lesser value does not mean no value and no moral obligation, only lower order of priority.

In Isaiah 40 we are told God has always had knowledge, understanding, and a sense of justice.[95] This means before He created anything, when only He existed, He understood and submitted to moral law. Since there was only one object to perceive—Himself—His intuition of value must have been a perception of His own being. This perception also would have had no beginning, existing as long as He has existed, since it is a function of His being and spiritual capacities.

This is not an unusual idea, as we can also perceive our own value, and the attending sense of obligation to our own well-being. We perceive our fingers as valuable, and experience an obligation to not chop them off. We know God believes He is more valuable than any other being in the universe, because He commands us to put His well-being before that of all other beings. He commanded, "You shall love the Lord your God," and, "You shall have no other gods before Me." The only way He could make those commands is if He knows His value demands it. Not only that, but it is actually good for us to put Him first, since all of His commands are "for our good."

If God's eternal perception of His own value imposed on Him a sense of responsibility to choose His highest well-being, then His own being imposes on Him a moral obligation. Thus, God is not above moral law, and the law He follows originates as a function of His own being and personality. There are a number of verses in the Bible describing intuition as a capacity of spirit,[96] so it is not speculation to assume God, as a Spirit, is able to intuit His own value, and as a result perceives a sense of moral obligation.

This same function is hinted at in the passage in Romans 2 stating that those who have not heard "the law" are "a law" unto

---

[95] Isaiah 40:14.
[96] Mark 2:8 ; Job 32:8 ; Romans 8:16 ; I Corinthians 2:11.

themselves. They show the "work of the law" written in their hearts. This appears to be a statement that any being created in the image of God, having His characteristics (albeit finite), will perceive the same moral law (the law of love) that originates in the nature and personality of God as a function of His capacities.

This also means moral law is not arbitrary, i.e. dependent on the choices of the moral being, but is absolute, springing from the very nature of the being. Rather than obligation originating from choices, the choices of a being will be judged by the previously perceived moral obligation. If this is true, then both God and man are obligated by their very natures to follow the law of love—God because of Who He is, and man, because he is created in the image of God.

One very interesting idea, though speculative, is the origination of moral law in light of the unity and diversity in the Godhead. If God were only one "simple" being (in the metaphysical sense), and not three persons, He would only have His own subjective intuition to validate His law to other moral beings. But because He is three as well as one, the members of the Godhead can both subjectively and objectively verify that the law God follows is not only right for Him, but for any other moral being (and He does so with infinite understanding!). Thus, He commands us to live by the same law of love He follows, and He is absolutely right to do so.

The answer to the question of whether or not God submits to a moral law also determines how we will judge the actions of God as He relates to other moral beings. Abraham assumed this to be true when he asked God, "Shall not the Judge of all the earth do right?"[97] Either He can do whatever He wants, and whatever He does is right, or He must also follow moral law, and He is thus obligated to do what is right, even though it may not be what He would like to do under the circumstances. In other words, if God has moral obligation, then there will be times in His interaction with other moral beings, that He will not be morally free to do what He would like to do, but must follow His own law, and do what is right. This means God can face a moral dilemma, and must decide which of two (or several) options will be better, even though He may not want to do either (or any).

---

[97] Genesis 18:25.

Probably the clearest example of this is God's will that all people be saved. He wants all people to know Him and have eternal life. But as important as eternal life is, God will not force anyone to have a relationship with Him. Taking away a person's will, even for the sake of salvation, is not something God is willing to do. He wants them to be saved, but he is unable (morally) to force them, against their will, to repent and believe.

At this point, some people might object, because they cannot see how God could face a dilemma. Well, it is not because some finite being can limit God, but because God is committed to fulfilling His own law of love. Thus, God often cannot (in the moral sense, not metaphysical) do what He would like to do, because His own law will not allow Him to do so. God faces dilemmas because of His commitment to His own free will, and the free will of man, and not because any finite being controls Him. To put it another way, God brought limitations on Himself by creating finite beings in His own image.

There are really only two ways to look at this: 1) either God had no law to which He was responsible, but could do anything He wanted with respect to Job, or 2) God has moral obligations to which He must submit (the law of love), and as a result had to do what was right in Job's case, even if it meant God could not do what He wanted. If the first alternative is true, then the book of Job is only a record of what God did, when He could have done anything else He wanted. This could raise serious questions about God's justice and goodness in His treatment of Job. But if the second alternative is true, which the Scriptures seem to support, then God had to do what was right toward every being involved in the situation, and so could not just do whatever He wanted. This moral self-limitation of God sets the stage for the drama of the book of Job.

Job and the Sovereignty of God

Some Christians might argue since God is sovereign, there is really no point in explaining Job's suffering. "God can do whatever He pleases," they reason, "so if He wanted to let Satan attack Job, and wanted Job to suffer, that is His business. God is sovereign."

If God has His own moral law to which He must submit, then what does it mean for God to be sovereign? Though this word appears infrequently in the Scriptures, one could argue since the concept is there, the word could still be useful.[98] If we are going to use the word, then we should at least give it a biblical definition.

One good way to define something is to first define what it is not. Here are a few ways the word "sovereign" has been defined that are not in line with what the Scriptures teach about the nature and character of God.

1. **Sovereignty is not** the absolute predestination of every event in human history. Though some theologies teach God determined what every event in history would be from all eternity past, this does not stand up to biblical or logical scrutiny.

The Bible is full of examples of events God did not plan or ever want to happen. But if God had predestined all events in history, then He would not (or could not) object to their occurrence. That God was grieved by man's sin, even to the point of being sorry He had created man,[99] indicates He had not planned man's rebellion. How could He be grieved over something He had been planning for all eternity?

Logically, if God had planned every event in history, then every choice of every person would also have been determined by God. This means choices a person assumes are truly free are actually predetermined by God, and as such cannot be a result

---

[98] It is used only twice with reference to God in the *New American Standard Bible*—once in Psalm 103:19 to mean "kingdom" and once in I Timothy 6:15 to mean "mighty one" or "powerful one."

Although the New International Version of the Bible uses the word "sovereign" over 200 times, mostly in the phrase "Sovereign Lord," this is a misrepresentation of the words. The Hebrew words here—Adonai Yaweh—are both properly translated "Lord," but saying "Lord, Lord" is a little awkward (though the LXX does this in Greek). So the words are often translated differently in English. "The Lord, Yaweh," would give a proper impression of the phrase, but using the word "Sovereign" as an adjective to modify "Lord" is an imposition of a theological position into the translation.

[99] Genesis 6.

of their will. This would also imply the person is not responsible for those "choices," since they did not originate with him.[100]

And what about Satan and Job? If God had determined ahead of time that Satan would attack Job, that God would give Satan permission, and that Job would suffer, what does this imply about the goodness and justice of God? You could look at it two ways. Either these events prove God is not a God of love, and cares nothing for justice, or the events have no meaning whatsoever, since what appear to be significant choices were only events predetermined by God anyway.

2. **Sovereignty is not** the absolute control of every event in human history. "God has everything under control" declares the bumper sticker. But I wonder if the unbelievers in the car behind think He is doing such a good job. What about the wars, the rapes, the deformed children, and all the other evil and suffering He is supposed to be controlling? Some people may derive comfort from the thought that God is controlling every event in their lives, but then who is responsible when bad things happen?

If God controlled the events in Job's life, then his suffering was God's fault, because He could have stopped the suffering, but did not.

3. **Sovereignty is not** a guarantee everything that happens is God's will. The theology "everything that happens is the will of God" is closely tied to the idea of absolute predestination. If everything is His will, then He must have chosen everything that happens, which is the same as predestination.

What is biblical sovereignty then? It is the rulership of God over everything. "The Lord has established His throne in the heavens, and His sovereignty rules over all."[101] He rules over the non-living creation through laws of cause and effect. He rules over animals through laws of instinct. And He rules over moral beings, those with a free will, with moral laws. He is the Ruler of all, and will bring every action into judgment for punishment or reward.

---

[100] The argument some people make that a person's choices are both free *and* determined by God is both verbal and logical absurdity. I have a full treatment of this kind of logic in my book, *Does God Know the Future?* (Xulon Press, 2002).
[101] Psalm 103:19.

But moral beings under His dominion are free to keep or break His law.

When events take place under His rulership that are not in line with His will, does this mean He is no longer sovereign? No, it does not. The sheriff of a county does not lose his position as sheriff because a county resident breaks into a house to steal a television set. Unlike the sheriff, though, God can and will bring every choice into judgment.

When Satan attacked Job, God did not lose His sovereignty. God remained the Ruler of all, and Satan will pay one day for his mistreatment of Job. But God could not justly stop the events without violating the wills of the beings involved. God's sovereignty includes the freedom of His subjects to disobey His loving rulership.

An Outline of the Book of Job

It is easy to admire and enjoy the beautiful poetry in Job, or become mentally engrossed with the complicated arguments of the different speakers. For our purposes, though, the general thrust of the story is more important, so an overview of the book will be helpful as a backdrop for the discussion.

The Prologue:
Section 1: Chapters 1-2 - A behind-the-scenes look at the reason for Job's suffering

The Discourses:
Section 2: Chapters 3-31 - Job's discourses with his three "comforters"

Section 3: Chapters 32-37 - Elihu's discourse with Job

Section 4: Chapters 38-41 - God's answer to Job (with a short response from Job in 40:3-5)

The Epilogue:
Section 5: Chapter 42:1-6 - Job's response to God

Section 6: Chapter 42:7-9 - God's response to Job's comforters

Section 7: Chapter 42:10-17 - Job's restoration

The book could be outlined in many ways, but this brief description will serve for the arguments about why Job suffered as an innocent party.

The Prologue

The first two chapters of Job provide the spiritual, philosophical, and theological undergirding for the message of the book. Before discussing the content of the first two chapters, it would be good to address the authorship of the book of Job. Theories abound, but they basically fall into just a few categories.

First, either the book of Job is part of the Word of God, or it is only so much interesting fiction. If it is just fiction, then there would be no reason to discuss it as if it portrayed a series of real events in history. The lessons portrayed in a work of fiction could be of some use, perhaps as a metaphor about life in general, but would not carry anywhere near the import of the inspired Word of God.[102]

Second, Job could be the author of the whole book.[103] If he wrote all of the book, then he eventually received a revelation of what was happening "behind the scenes" in his life. He may have written the Prologue and Epilogue after the Discourses. If he did, that would mean he received understanding of his suffering after the whole event was over.[104]

This could have affected Job's life in a number of ways, one of which would be his realization that he was mistaken in some of his statements. For example, when he declared after the first

---

[102] I suppose another option might be that the story is true, but not inspired by the Holy Spirit. In that case, however, one would need to ask where the author got his/her understanding of what was happening in the spiritual world. The events of the first two chapters require information about events in the spiritual realm, so which spirit communicated the "behind-the-scenes" story to the author?

[103] With the exception, of course, of his epitaph in the last verse.

[104] Some might ask why, if Job wrote the book, it is written in the third person. This is not unusual for writings of that time. Nor is it unusual for the Scriptures. After all, Moses wrote the first five books of the Bible, the bulk of which is a record of his own life, and yet he wrote it in the third person.

test, "The Lord gave and the Lord has taken away,"[105] he may have eventually learned he was wrong. Actually, the Lord gave and Satan took away. It is true Job said this, but what he said was not true about his circumstances. That may have been quite a revelation for Job, if he wrote the whole book.

Third, Job could be the author of the poetic portions (the Discourses), but not of the prose portions at the beginning and end of the book (the Prologue and Epilogue). In that case, someone else was given understanding of what was happening in the spiritual world, and why Job suffered as he did. Given this scenario, Job may have never had understanding as to why he suffered.

Fourth, there is the possibility someone other than Job wrote the whole book. In that case, we must assume though Job was not the author, the Holy Spirit inspired someone to record Job's story so it could be part of the body of God's Word.

I will be proceeding on the assumptions that the book of Job is the Word of God, and that Job wrote the whole book, though the latter assumption is not absolutely necessary to make sense of the message of the book.

Chapter 1 - A Glimpse Behind the Veil

Verses one through five of chapter one describe Job, his character, his children, his possessions, and his care for his seven sons and three daughters.

Job is described as "blameless, upright, fearing God, and turning away from evil." Though this could be taken as just the author's opinion of Job, or a report of Job's reputation, we learn later this is actually God's opinion. Job also had many possessions, including "very many" servants, and he was known as "the greatest of all the men of the east."

Job was not concerned with only his own righteousness, though, as the narrative describes his sacrifices for his children. Job was so concerned about their relationship to God, he offered burnt offerings for them on the basis of *"Perhaps* my sons have sinned."

---

[105] Job 1:21.

It is against the backdrop of this kind of righteousness that God reveals what was happening "behind the scenes" in the spiritual world.

Satan's Challenge and God's Moral Dilemma

In the span of seven verses in chapter one (6-12), we are given insight into the reason for Job's sufferings. Let's take a close look at each verse.

In verse six we read:

Now there was a day when the sons of God came to present themselves before the Lord, and Satan also came among them.

"Now there was a day." We are not told which day this was, but it was probably a short time before Job's troubles began.

"The sons of God" are hard to identify, though it is commonly assumed these were angelic beings. The phrase is not used enough in the Scriptures to state definitely what it means, but since they could come before God, and Satan, who is a fallen spiritual being, had access to this place "before the Lord," it would seem the assumption they were angels is compelling. Another evidence for this is the presence of the "sons of God" at the creation of the earth.[106]

Although an exact number is not given, if the "sons of God" were angels, there is a great probability there were vast numbers of beings present. In the book of Revelation we are told there were "myriads of myriads" and "thousands of thousands" of angels who gathered before God.[107] In Greek, the word "myriad" is used literally for ten thousand, but it is also often used for a vast, incomprehensible number. But even using the literal definition, "myriads of myriads" would be 100 million, and "thousands of thousands" would be 1 million, so the lowest number might be 101 million angels. But since this word is also used figuratively for

---

[106] Job 38:4-7.
[107] Revelation 5:11. See also Numbers 10:36 ; Psalm 68:17 ; Daniel 7:10 ; Hebrews 12:22.

even larger numbers, it could be there were many more millions of angels present, perhaps even billions.[108] The point is, though, that Satan and God were definitely not speaking in private. There were vast numbers of beings listening to their conversation.

Verse seven states:

And the Lord said to Satan, "From where do you come?" Then Satan answered the Lord and said, "From roaming about on the earth and walking around on it."

God asks Satan what seems to be a simple question, but there is far more here than meets the eye. Satan desires to be God, but can never attain that goal. Satan simply is not God by his very nature, and never can be. Paul told the Galatians, "However at that time, when you did not know God, you were slaves to those which *by nature are no gods.*"[109] What determines if a being is God or not? This is determined by the nature of the being. Thus, when God asked Satan where he came from, this was a subtle reminder to Satan that he cannot be everywhere, as God can, and so Satan can never attain godhood. God forced him to admit he was not God, and God did this before millions of other beings.

Though some may wonder about the wisdom of irritating Satan in this way, it was actually an act of kindness, both to Satan, and to the other "sons of God" who were listening. Satan needed to have his pride humbled by being reminded he is not now, and never will be, God. The other beings there were reminded of the truth that there is only one God, and He is the only being qualified to be the Governor of the whole creation. God's comparison of Satan's nature with His own was both loving and kind, though Satan probably reacted only in anger at the reminder.

---

[108] If we assume that phrases such as "their angels do always behold the face of their Father" and that angels are "spirits sent to minister to the heirs of salvation" mean that God prepared one angel for each possible human being, then the idea that there could be billions of angels is not really a stretch. Since God knew the earth could support billions of inhabitants, it may be that He prepared billions of angels to minister to them. This is speculation, of course, but not outside the realm of possibility.

[109] Galatians 4:8. See also Acts 17:29.

If we read quickly through this part of the passage to get to Satan's attack on Job, we might miss a very important aspect of the story. God did not start by comparing Satan to Job. God started by comparing Satan to Himself. And God did this in more than one way.

Verse eight tells us:

And the Lord said to Satan, "Have you considered My servant Job? For there is no one like him on the earth, a blameless and upright man, fearing God and turning away from evil."

Sometimes we are so astounded by God's description of Job, we miss the question God has for Satan. "Have you *considered* My servant Job?" Have you thought about him? It is easy to miss, but God is again comparing Satan's nature to His own. If Satan had to consider Job—to think about him—this means Job was not always an object of Satan's knowledge. To put this another way, God was reminding Satan he is not able to know all things, that is, he is not omniscient. Again, Satan's nature does not qualify him to be God.

The Lord is just in all His ways, and kind in all His deeds. And these comparisons God made were no exception. God was just, kind, loving, and wise in His pointing out to Satan, and that before the other angelic beings, that Satan by his very nature is not God.

Then comes the amazing declaration Job is unique in all the world for being blameless, upright, revering God, and turning away from evil. These same words are already recorded in the first verse of the chapter, but there they are the words of the author. Here they are coming from the mouth of God Himself. As amazing as it seems, Job must have had these qualities. God could not be mistaken about the character of a human being.

God "bragged" about Job before Satan and perhaps a few million other beings. But why would God do this? What purpose could it serve? Actually, Job's case was not an isolated incident. Rather, it is just one example of a general principle God uses in his dealings with spiritual beings. Ephesians 3:10 explains this principle:

... in order that the manifold wisdom of God might now be made known through the church to the rulers and the authorities in the heavenly places.

How does God make His wisdom known to spiritual beings? He does it *through the church*. God uses the body of Christ—those who are following Him and living as He does—as an example of how finite beings should live. Job's case was not unusual. God was following His general method of teaching His wisdom to spiritual beings when He compared Job's righteous character to Satan's rebellious lifestyle.

In essence, God was saying, "Do you see Job, Satan? He is just a human being, a finite being like you, and yet He follows me completely. You could do the same, so there is no excuse for your rebellion. He is living as I do, in love, and you should be living that way too."

It is also important not to forget the millions of beings who were listening to this exchange. God praises Job for his character, and by implication compares that character to Satan's behavior. In doing this, God is also reinforcing in the minds of the "sons of God" that the way they were living, loving and serving God as Job did, was the right way to live. The magnitude of this is staggering. God said He was living in love, Job was following His example, and the "sons of God" were also living as God was, submitting to the law of love. All of this must have been extremely annoying to Satan.

Then comes the crucial question. Verse nine records Satan's objection:

Then Satan answered the Lord, "Does Job fear God for nothing?"

To paraphrase this, Satan is asking, "Do you think Job fears You just because it is the right thing to do? No! He fears You because of what he can get out of You. You protect him, bless the work of his hands, and help him increase his wealth and possessions. No, his reverence for You is motivated by selfishness." Satan attacked Job's character by questioning his motives.

Charles Finney, and authors of his time, had a very concise and helpful way of referring to what Satan was describing here. They wrote of "benevolence,"[110] a word coming from two Latin roots— "bene," meaning "well or good," and "volens," meaning "wish or choose." Thus, they described benevolence as wishing or choosing the well-being, or good, of another. They often described love as true benevolence—the act of choosing for the highest well-being of God, human beings, or any part of His created order.

Along with this they described two reasons for making this choice to love. One was to make the choice just because it is the right choice to make. This they called "disinterested benevolence." That is, the person does what is right with no regard for his own personal outcome. He is not interested in the results in his own life. He lives in benevolence (love) just because it is the right way to live. If he is rewarded, that is just the result of his actions. On the other hand, if he does what is right, and suffers for it, he will live that way anyway, because it is the right way to live.

But Satan was accusing Job of "interested benevolence," claiming Job only lived righteously because of the rewards God lavished on his life. Satan describes these blessings in verse ten:

"Have You not made a hedge about him and his house and all that he has, on every side? You have blessed the work of his hands, and his possessions have increased in the land."

Amazingly, in his question, Satan compares himself to God, though it is not obvious at first glance. How did Satan know there was a hedge around Job, his house, and all he had? This knowledge probably came from trying unsuccessfully to attack Job in all these areas. But what is really revealing, here, is that Satan could not touch Job. This means he was admitting God had the power to protect Job from anything Satan could throw at him. By asking this question, Satan was admitting God was omnipotent, and he was

---

[110] *Lectures on Systematic Theology*, by Charles G. Finney (London: William Tegg and Co., 85, Queen Street, Cheapside, 1851), Lecture II, section 11 and Lecture V, section 16.

not. Again, the comparison of God's nature with Satan's proves Satan is not God.

I am going to digress here, just a little, to give a practical example of how this "doctrine of Satan" blessed the life of a young woman.

Praise God for a Good Doctrine of Satan!

One of the female students in the missionary school where I was teaching asked if I could counsel her about a persistent problem in her life.

When we got together, I noticed a distinct feeling of heaviness in the room. This sense of evil was obviously coming from the young woman. The longer we talked, the heavier the oppression became. The experience was very disturbing.

The woman shared she had once worked with a stage magician, and it was during this time she had begun to feel a darkness enter her life. Even though she had given her life to Christ, the feeling of oppression just would not leave. She had prayed to be released from occult bondage, but that had not brought her any relief.

As she talked, I could tell from her description of Satan and evil spirits that she had an unbiblical idea of their power and knowledge. I thought a good starting place might be to show her how God revealed Satan's nature in the book of Job.

"God asked Satan where he had come from," I shared, "which means Satan cannot be everywhere at one time like God can. He is not omnipresent. God also asked Satan if he had thought about Job, which means Satan does not know everything—he is not omniscient. And Satan had tried to attack Job and his possessions, but God protected him. That means Satan is not all-powerful, or omnipotent. Satan is just a finite being who is in rebellion against God. He is not an evil version of God. There is just no comparison between the Creator, and one of his rebellious finite creatures."

I could see on the woman's face she was carefully contemplating what she had just heard. "Do you mean," she asked slowly, her face revealing a sudden enlightenment, "that if Satan is in Hong Kong right now, that he can't be here too, and he doesn't know what I am thinking?"

"That's correct," I said. "He can only be in one place at a time, and his knowledge is finite."

All we could do was stare at each other as we both felt the power of the dark oppression break and then vanish from the room. The feeling of lightness was overwhelming. The truth from God's word had broken and driven out the heaviness plaguing this young woman for years.

The young woman was free, and it was all because of a good doctrine of Satan.

Does Job Fear God for Nothing?

It is important to understand when Satan accused Job of a selfish motivation for loving God, Satan was not just accusing Job. Satan was questioning the way Job was living, but along with Job, Satan was questioning the way God was living, and also all of the beings who were there listening to this conversation. God lives in disinterested benevolence. Job was following God's example, living in love, just because it is the right way to live. The "sons of God" who were there were also following God's example of righteousness. Thus, when Satan accused Job of selfishness, he was indirectly accusing God and the "sons of God" of unrighteousness as well.

"I'll prove it to You," Satan gloated. "If You just take away Your blessings from his life, he will curse You to Your face." As verse eleven puts it:

"But put forth Your hand now and touch all that he has; he will surely curse You to Your face."

It is right here, between verses eleven and twelve, that the whole drama of Job begins. It is also here that a person's view of God's relationship to moral law determines how he will interpret the whole message of the book. If God can do whatever He wants, and has no law by which He must live, then His decision to let Satan attack Job was purely arbitrary. If God could have just as easily said, "No, you can't touch him," then one would have to question the goodness, the justice, and the wisdom of God in giving Satan permission to attack Job. If, however, God must live by the law of love, and do what is just toward all free-will beings in every case, then the story is completely different.

Let's suppose God must live according to His own moral law. What if God had said, "No, I won't let you touch him"? Satan could have turned on his heel, shouted, "Aha! Won my point!" and departed, leaving behind millions of beings wondering if Job, God, and they were all living correctly. Refusing permission would have caused far more damage to God's rulership over the "sons of God" than any failure of Job could produce. These beings, whoever they were, would always have to question whether or not God's assessment of Job was correct, whether or not it was good for Job to live as God lived, and whether or not they, the "sons of God," were living the right way. Beyond all of this, if God withheld permission, He would slander His own character, as He brought into question the way He lives—following the law of love unselfishly.

God was facing a moral dilemma. On the one hand He could say, "Yes, you can touch him," and suffer the agony of watching Job suffer as an innocent party. Or He could say, "No, you can't touch him," and cause great damage in the lives of millions of beings. Evidently the better of the two options was to let Satan touch Job, rather than cause upheaval in His government over all these moral beings. The point was not if Job would respond correctly, and it was certainly not if God had the power to stop Satan. God had to decide which was more just, loving, and wise— let Job suffer, and uphold His government for the good of other moral beings, or spare Job, and bring detriment to the lives of millions of free-will agents. Morally, God had only one way He could go. He had to let Satan attack Job.

Some people have great difficulty accepting that God could have a moral dilemma, and have to let someone suffer, rather than deny that person their free will. And yet this happens many times every day. Every time a person dies and goes to hell, God is faced with a moral dilemma. Should He make the person love him, and spare them the suffering of hell, or should He allow the person to go to hell, but preserve their freedom and significance as a being? Evidently God thinks it is better for the person to suffer in hell eternally, than to take away their free will. We know this is not what God wants to do, because God says He "has no pleasure in the death of the wicked."[111] Rather, this is what God must do, if He is going to be just to the person's free will.

Yes, God faced a moral dilemma because of the choices of Satan—let Job suffer, or cause even more damage by saying, "No." An upcoming section will explain how God Himself blames Satan for the moral dilemma, and declares Satan to be the reason for Job's trials.

Verse twelve says:

> Then the Lord said to Satan, "Behold, all that he has is in your power, only do not put forth your hand on him." So Satan departed from the presence of the Lord.

Why would God limit the destruction Satan wanted to bring on Job? Because morally He could. Satan only accused Job of selfishness as related to his possessions ("all that he has"). He would later attack Job's character based on his health, and God would be forced to let Satan touch Job's body. But for now, following the exact accusation Satan made, God only had to allow Satan to destroy Job's possessions.

We then read from verse thirteen to the end of the chapter (verse 22) Satan either took or destroyed Job's oxen, donkeys, sheep, camels, and servants. Satan then killed Job's children. All that was left was a couple of servants to bring Job the news. One rather unhelpful servant even ventured to accuse God of destroying the sheep and servants.

In verse 21 we read that Job said, "The Lord gave and the Lord has taken away." At the time this was how Job understood what was happening. He was mistaken, of course, and would later realize what he said was wrong. God had given, and Satan had taken away.

For some people this may not seem like a big point, but it can be crucial to a person's relationship with God. At many funerals the phrase is given as a reason a person has died. "The Lord gave and the Lord has taken away." Hearing this explanation of a

---

[111] Ezekiel 18:23.

relative's death, many people have come to question the love and justice of God. Some of these people have turned away from God altogether, preferring to have no God, than a God who takes away a loved one, seemingly without reason.[112]

But let's think about this. How many people did God ever want to die? Did He not warn Adam and Eve not to eat of the tree of the knowledge of good and evil for this very reason? He commanded them not to eat of it lest they die. So when someone dies, did God want that to happen? No, He did not.

Many objections can be offered to counter this argument, but they all only prove the point. Has God sometimes killed people? Yes. Has God sometimes commanded people to kill other people? Yes. And yet God says He has no pleasure in the death of the wicked. This only proves the point God faces moral dilemmas all the time. He must allow people to rebel against Him, and then must punish them for their rebellion. He does not want them to go to hell, but must allow them to do so. Even though He has judged people for their rebellion by killing them, He did not want to, but had to do it in order to be just.

Job's situation was not one of the guilty suffering punishment, but of the innocent suffering under the attack of Satan. We know God gave, but Satan took away, because God had already declared Job righteous, and the Scriptures tell us Satan was the one who destroyed Job's possessions and killed his children.[113] Job's reaction was reasonable, given the circumstances, but if he wrote the Prologue, he eventually learned he was wrong.

Chapter 2 - The Second Test

After Satan tested Job by destroying his possessions and children, the Bible records there was another day when the "sons of God" came before the Lord, and Satan came among them.

---

[112] It is good to keep in mind that just because we know it was not God, but Satan, who killed Job's children, this does not mean it is always Satan who kills people. In fact, it will usually be some other reason the person died, such as disease, natural disaster, human malice, an accident, etc.

[113] Though we do not read directly in verses 13-21 that Satan was behind the destruction of Job's possessions, God does blame Satan for those actions in Job 2:3.

Verse one of chapter two states:

> Again there was a day when the sons of God came to present themselves before the Lord, and Satan also came among them to present himself before the Lord.

The Scriptures do not tell us how often the "sons of God" appear before the Lord, but obviously Satan could not refrain from attending this meeting. He had destroyed Job's property and children, and still Job would not speak improperly about God. Evidently, Satan did not want to miss an opportunity to continue his attack on Job.

Then the Lord asked the "annoying" question again. Satan's answer was the same as the first time. Verse two says:

> And the Lord said to Satan, "Where have you come from?" Then Satan answered the Lord and said, "From roaming about on the earth, and walking around on it."

The Lord's next comment to Satan can be divided into three distinct parts. First, God repeats His opinion of Job's character. Second, God acknowledges Job's correct response during Satan's first attack. And third, God places the blame for Job's suffering squarely on Satan's shoulders.

Verse three reads like this:

> And the Lord said to Satan, "Have you considered My servant Job? For there is no one like him on the earth, a blameless and upright man fearing God and turning away from evil. And he still holds fast his integrity, although you incited Me against him, to ruin him without cause."

The last part of this verse, together with Satan's accusation "Does Job fear God for nothing?" gives the complete picture of why Job suffered as an innocent party. Satan accused Job of serving God for what he could get out of Him. Because of the circumstances, God could not justly withhold permission for Satan to destroy Job's possessions and children. Job responded correctly, maintaining his integrity. Then, when Satan came back for a second run at Job, God placed the blame squarely on Satan for Job's suffering.

A close look at the words in God's explanation are very revealing:

- you
- incited Me
- against him
- to ruin him
- without a cause

When God says "you," of course He is addressing Satan. This is simple enough to understand.

But then God says "incited Me," which is not as easy to comprehend. This Hebrew word, *suth*, is also translated as "divert," "entice," "induce," "mislead," "move," "persuade," and "stir up" in other places in the Scriptures.[114] The common theme in these translations is the word "incite" is used when one person is doing something to another person in order to elicit, or even coerce, a particular response. Thus, God is saying to Satan that he (Satan) did something to God by the way he acted, in order to force God into doing something He would not have done otherwise. Of course, this "forcing" had to be moral, and not physical, since Satan could not have forced God to do anything by any physical (or metaphysical) means.

Next, the "incitement," or "moving" if you will, was "against him," that is, against Job. When Satan presented God with a moral dilemma, God could have ruled *for Job*, not allowing him to suffer, or *against Job*, allowing him to suffer. Because the ramifications of ruling for Job would be more damaging than ruling against him, God was "forced," morally, to allow Job to suffer.

The really crucial word in this whole statement is the infinitive Hebrew verb "to ruin" (literally, "to swallow up"). In this case the verb also has an object—Job. Satan incited God against Job in order to ruin Job.

---

[114] See the Appendix for a list of verses where *suth* is used in the Scriptures.

The real question here, though, is whether the verb "to ruin" is referring to God's ruining Job, or Satan's ruining Job. Unfortunately, many people have supposed the verb is referring to God, when there is no good reason to interpret the statement that way. Though the verb is an infinitive, and could be read either way, the context does not warrant saying God ruined Job. Who went out from God's presence and destroyed Job's possessions and children? Satan did. Who struck Job with boils from the top of his head to the bottom of his feet? Satan did. We do not read anywhere in the book of Job that God attacked Job.[115] Thus, when it says "to ruin him," it would be best understood as meaning "so that you could ruin him."

The last phrase, "without a cause," is literally "for no reason" in the Hebrew. God, from His perspective, declares there was no reason for Job to suffer. First, God did not have anything to prove about Himself. Second, Job did not need to be tested to develop some kind of character quality. As far as God was concerned, Job was already blameless and upright. Third, God had nothing to prove to Satan. This means the only reason Job suffered was because of Satan's unmitigated hatred against the human race.

I have encountered many explanations as to why God *allowed* Job to suffer (or even *caused* Job to suffer, in some cases), but I have never seen any explanation stating God did it for no reason whatsoever. Yet God Himself says Job was ruined "for no reason." This is another good indication Satan was completely to blame for Job's suffering, and God had no part in it, other than He was forced morally to allow Satan to attack Job. It also gives us good reason to interpret the infinitive "to ruin him" as "in order to ruin him" or "so that you could ruin him."

If we put all these phrases together, we could say God explains the situation as:

He still holds fast his integrity, although you put Me in a moral dilemma, where I could not justly withhold permission from you, so that you could destroy him without any reason.

---

[115] For those who are very familiar with the story, I will address later the idea that God had brought evil on Job (42:11).

In Job 2:3, God gives us the definitive reason Job suffered. Satan, by his free will, posed a moral dilemma for God, and God could not justly withhold permission from Satan to attack Job. Job suffered because of the malicious intent of a fallen spiritual being. There was no great mystery to Job's suffering, and it certainly was not God's idea. God blamed Satan for Job's suffering, so that must be the truth.

Verses four and five read:

Satan answered the LORD and said, "Skin for skin! Yes, all that a man has he will give for his life. However, put forth Your hand now, and touch his bone and his flesh; he will curse You to Your face."

This is the same kind of accusation Satan made before the first test. He is claiming if God removes His protection from Job, and allows Satan to touch his flesh, Job will curse God. That would then prove Job was serving God for what He could give him (or, in interested benevolence).

Thus, we read in verse six:

So the Lord said to Satan, "Behold, he is in your power, only spare his life."

Again, God was in a moral dilemma. And again, God was forced to grant Satan permission. During the first test, Satan accused Job based on Job's possessions, so God was able to limit the damage to Job's possessions and children. In this second test, Satan claims Job will curse God if his health is removed. Thus, God was "incited" morally to allow Satan to touch Job's body. Since any relevant point would be lost if Job were dead, however, God had the moral right to forbid Satan from taking Job's life.

Then, in verse seven, it states:

Then Satan went out from the presence of the Lord, and smote Job with sore boils from the sole of his foot to the crown of his head.

The story continues with Job sitting in ashes, scraping off his boils with pieces of broken clay pot. Job's wife, probably through sympathy for Job, suggests he curse God. Maybe that way God will kill him, and Job's sufferings will end. Job's answer is another mistaken statement about God's involvement in his plight. "Shall we indeed accept good from God and not accept adversity?" As with his other statement about the Lord's "taking away," Job probably understood later his adversity was not God's doing.

Chapter two ends with the arrival of Job's friends—Eliphaz the Temanite, Bildad the Shuhite, and Zophar the Naamathite. When they saw Job, they wept, tore their robes, and threw dust in the air. Then they sat down with Job and were silent for seven days. Though we often look upon them as "miserable comforters" because of their accusations, still, it is an indication of the great friendship and respect they had for Job, that they would sit in silence for a whole week to sympathize with him.

The discourses begin in chapter three.

The Discourses

Though the discourses comprise the majority of the book of Job, they are actually easier to summarize than the first two chapters. They consist mostly of exchanges between Job and his comforters, with a discourse by Elihu toward the end, and then God's message to Job from the whirlwind.

Eliphaz, Bildad, and Zophar tried repeatedly to suggest because he was suffering, Job must have done something wrong. Job responded each time that he knew of nothing he had done to warrant such treatment. Both sides assumed, of course, that it was God who was attacking Job. This should be a significant lesson to all of us who try to comfort those who are suffering. If it is not obvious, we must be careful not to assume the source of someone else's suffering. What will we do if we are proven wrong in the end?

Job's "comforters" presented him with only one argument throughout their discourses, and their argument is based on flawed logic. Yet many people apply this fallacy to the sufferings of others, and sometimes to their own suffering. Once we see the logic laid out, we quickly understand how the comforters did not speak what was right about God. The problem is this logic is couched in very flowery, impressive poetry, so it is easy to miss the argument in all the verbiage.

One simple way to present logical arguments is to give them in three steps: a major premise, a minor premise, and a conclusion. This series of statements is referred to as a syllogism. Here is an example of a simple syllogism:

If an animal is a cow, then that animal has four legs.
This animal is a cow.
Therefore, this animal has four legs.

All things being normal for the cow, this logic is sound. The first line is the major premise, the second line is the minor premise, and the third line is the conclusion.

In "logic shorthand" this argument takes the form:

If p, then q
p
Therefore q

So how were the comforters arguing? If their basic argument is distilled from all the eloquent descriptions, it looks like this:

If you are guilty, then bad things will happen to you.
Bad things are happening to you.
Therefore, you are guilty.

Although this looks very similar to the first argument about cows, it is not at all the same. Applied to cows, their logic would look like this:

If an animal is a cow, then that animal has four legs.
This animal has four legs.
Therefore, this animal is a cow.

What about horses? Do they have four legs? Yes, and yet they are not cows. It is easy enough to see this logic is flawed. Yet with Job's comforters, their argument is buried in so much beautiful vocabulary, it can be difficult to discern.

As far as the logical shorthand is concerned, the syllogism looks like this.

If p, then q
q
Therefore p

This logical fallacy is called "affirming the consequent." That means the "q" part of the first premise becomes the minor premise. When this happens, the conclusion of "p" does not logically follow.

Of course, the comforters were assuming absolute justice always happens in each person's life. They thought every evil deed will be punished, and every righteous action will be rewarded. Though God is just, the world is not quite this simple, so one could even question whether or not their major premise was true. The point is, though, they believed the world works this way, so they assumed it to be true.

What can we learn from their mistaken logic? Just as there are many animals besides cows with four legs, so there are many reasons a person can suffer, not just from being guilty of sin. Though God might be punishing someone for their sins, it cannot be automatically assumed in every case that if a person is suffering, then God is doing it.

It is interesting how often we apply this bad logic to our own lives. If we are suffering, we think we must have done something wrong. If we are blessed, we think we must be doing everything right. Yet, in a fallen world there are many reasons we can suffer that have nothing to do with our righteousness or holiness.

We can become ill just because our bodies are part of the fallen world. We can be stabbed on the street because we are preaching the Gospel. Having bad things happen does not automatically mean we have sinned and are being punished.

On the other hand, if we are being blessed, this does not mean we are living correctly. The Bible tells us "the goodness of God is meant to lead you to repentance."[116] Sometimes the Lord blesses us because He is trying to get us to repent. Life in the fallen world is not as simple as some people would like to portray it. There are many causes for suffering, and we should not assume the reason is personal moral evil, just because someone is experiencing adversity.

God's Message to Job

Before moving on to the Epilogue, and a couple of puzzling verses about Job's suffering, it might be good to look at God's message to Job from the whirlwind.

After all the accusations from Eliphaz, Bildad, Zophar, and Elihu, God finally responds to Job. While it is true God did not accuse Job of speaking improperly about Him, it is also interesting He did not praise Job, either. God commenced with, "Who is this that darkens counsel by words without knowledge?" God did not accuse Job of wrongdoing, but He reminded Job that speaking from a lack of knowledge does not produce good counsel.[117]

God proceeded to ask Job a very long string of questions about Job's knowledge and power. These questions were an indirect way of teaching Job the nature of God. Of course, as always, God's strategy was brilliant. Each question made Job see the greatness of God on the one hand, and his own smallness on the other. God seldom declared outright that He did something. Rather, he asked Job if he could do it, and by His question affirmed both that God could, and that Job could not.

In his discourses with his comforters, Job sometimes entertained the possibility God might be behind his suffering. "If it is not He, then who is it?"[118] he asked. Yet in all of his

---

[116] Romans 2:4.

[117] It is possible, that though God's message from the whirlwind was directed at Job, if the others there could hear God speaking, then God might have been instructing them also. Their "words without knowledge" definitely darkened their counsel, so God's questions could have had more than one recipient in view.

[118] Job 9:24.

contemplation and questions, he did not malign God's character. But since he allowed the possibility God could be behind his suffering, evidently God decided it would be good to correct his understanding. Remember: though God's tone sometimes appears to be sarcastic, God never accuses Job of any sin. On the contrary, He said Job spoke rightly of Him. And when Job "repented," it was not for sin, but for a lack of knowledge (more on that later).

The questions and descriptions God presented to Job fall into basically five categories—God's knowledge,[119] power,[120] location,[121] duration,[122] and ownership of the earth.[123] He also uses descriptions of two creatures, Behemoth and Leviathan, to make the point that if Job cannot handle them, then he obviously cannot compare himself to God.

As strange as it may seem at first, what God gave Job was exactly what he needed—an expanded revelation of the greatness of God. Though God could have simply explained He was not causing Job's suffering, and Satan was the culprit, this was not Job's greatest need. When we suffer, what we really need to know is God is aware of our suffering, He loves us, and He is great enough to take care of us no matter what happens. God met this need in Job through a barrage of questions aimed at teaching Job how small he was, and how great God is. In His love and wisdom toward us, God often meets our need rather than answering our questions. If we receive both, that is a special blessing.

In reading the exchange between God and Job, it is very important to keep in mind that a question is neither a statement, nor an accusation. When God asks Job, "Will the faultfinder contend with the Almighty? Let him who reproves God answer it," Job's answer was not to repent of sin, nor to venture an answer, but to acknowledge he was insignificant, and had no reply. The issue here was not sin, but knowledge.

---

[119] Job 38:2, 3b, 4b, 5a, 18, 20b, 21a, 33a, 37a ; 39:1, 2, 26 ; 40:1, 2, 4, 5, 7, 8.

[120] Job 38:8-11, 12, 25030, 31, 32, 33b, 34, 35, 36, 37b, 39-41 ; 39:5, 10, 19, 20, 27 ; 40: 4, 9, 10-14, 24 ; 41:1-9 (power of Leviathan), 10 (comparison of God with Leviathan), 12-34.

[121] Job 38:4a, 5b, 16, 17, 19, 20a, 22, 24.

[122] Job 38:4a, 21, 7.

[123] Job 41:11.

The Epilogue

As outlined previously, the Epilogue consists of three parts—Job's response to God, God's response to Job's comforters, and Job's restoration. This portion of Job can appear confusing at first, since we see Job "repenting," and his family consoling him "for all the evil the Lord had brought on him." But with a little careful inspection of the words themselves, and the context, these seeming difficulties can be resolved.

Job's Response to God

First, there is Job's response to God. He acknowledges God can do all things, and God's purpose cannot be thwarted. How else could Job respond, really? After God's message to him from the whirlwind, there was no other proper reaction.

Then Job quotes back to God His evaluation of Job's knowledge. "Who is this that hides counsel without knowledge?" By repeating this phrase, Job admits God's opinion of his lack of knowledge is accurate. Job then goes on to amplify God's assessment:

Therefore I have declared that which I did not understand, things too wonderful for me, which I did not know.

After his recognition of deficient knowledge, Job then asks God to instruct him. Job prays, "Hear, now, and I will speak; I will ask Thee, and do Thou instruct me." And why does Job need this instruction? It is because his information about God, which he thought was accurate, was proven to be deficient in light of an actual revelation of God Himself.

Then comes a statement that can seem very confusing, unless it is considered in the whole context of the book of Job:

I have heard of You by the hearing of the ear; But now my eye sees You; *Therefore I retract, And I repent in dust and ashes.* (emphasis mine)

Job thought he knew about God, but after God's revelation to him from the whirlwind, Job realized he was woefully deficient in true knowledge about the Almighty. He likens this lack in understanding about God to the difference between only hearing about someone, and then finally meeting the person face to face. No matter how much he had heard about God, actually seeing God showed him who God really was, and now Job needed to adjust his knowledge about the Lord.

So Job responds:

I retract (literally, I despise myself), and I repent in dust and ashes.

Because the word "repent" is used in our English translations, people jump to the conclusion Job must have been guilty of some sin, and he is finally ready to confess it. Yet this same word "repent" is used of God 36 times in the Bible.[124] When people see this word applied to God, they know it cannot mean God sinned, so it must be interpreted some other way in the context. The same is true of Job here. God said Job had not sinned, and there is no evidence in the entire book of Job that he did. So the word must be referring to something else.

The Hebrew word used for "repent" here is literally "to change the mind." When this literal definition is applied to God's actions, it makes perfect sense. For example, God was planning to destroy the nation of Israel, but when Moses interceded, God "changed His mind" (repented), and did not destroy the people.[125] We understand God was changing His mind, and not repenting of a sin He had committed.

Job needed to "change his mind" about what he knew of God. When Job "repents," he does not mention any sin of which he is guilty, but is acknowledging he needs to change his understanding

---

[124] Genesis 6:6, 7; Exodus 32:12, 14; Numbers 23:19; Deuteronomy 32:36; Judges 2:18; I Samuel 15:11, 29, 35; II Samuel 24:16; I Chronicles 21:15; Psalms 90:13; 106:45; 110:4; 135:14; Jeremiah 4:28; 15:6; 18:8, 10; 20:16; 26:3, 13, 19; 42:10; Ezekiel 24:14; Hosea 11:8; 13:14; Joel 2:13, 14; Amos 7:3, 6; Jonah 3:9, 10; 4:2; Zechariah 8:14.
[125] Exodus 32:14.

of the Almighty. The entire context is about knowledge, and not sin.

As with many situations, we see God bringing something wonderful out of a horrible circumstance. Satan tried to destroy Job so he could accuse Job, God, and the Sons of God of doing what is right for selfish motives. Satan not only failed, due to Job's character, but God used the situation to reveal Himself to Job. This does not mean Job's suffering was good, or that God planned it to teach Job something. It simply means God is able to produce good things in the midst of terrible circumstances, if those involved respond correctly to God.

God's Response to Job's Comforters

The second part of the Epilogue is God's response to Job's comforters. In spite of all their fancy explanations about Job's suffering, God became angry with them, because they did not speak what was right about God, as Job did. No matter how tough Job's questions were, he did not blame God for his situation when he had no evidence God was at fault. His statements can look at times as if he is questioning God's actions, but since God said he spoke what is right, then we must accept God's evaluation of Job's words. They were correct, even though they were based on a lack of knowledge on Job's part.

The comforters' basic argument was if you are suffering, you must have done something wrong, and God is punishing you for it. Since God rebuked them, telling them they did not speak rightly of Him, then this argument must be incorrect. As we have seen, there are many reasons people can suffer in this fallen world. The judgment of God is only one of them. Coming under attack from evil spiritual beings is another. Their assumption that God was behind Job's suffering was mistaken, and we have God's affirmation their reasonings were fallacious.

Even so, God allowed them to offer sacrifices, and directed Job to pray for them, so the Lord would not deal with them according to their "folly." When Job prayed for his friends, God accepted him, and began restoring the things Satan had stolen from Job's life.

God's Restoration of Job

The third and final portion of the Epilogue is the account of Job's restoration. It begins with Job's prayer for his friends, and God's increasing twofold all of Job's possessions.

In verse eleven we read Job's "brothers, and all his sisters, and all who had known him before" came back to him, and ate bread with him. One might be prompted to ask, "And just where were his brothers, sisters, and those who knew him all the time he was suffering?" Although we could wonder why they did not assist Job during his ordeal, we should be understanding of their position. It is often very difficult emotionally to be a relative of a person who is suffering. This is even more stressful if there is nothing you can do for your loved one who is in pain. Thus, we should be sympathetic with their plight, as well as Job's, even as we wonder, "Where were you all this time? Not even a visit?"

Then, still in verse eleven, we read this curious statement:

"...and they consoled him and comforted him for all the evil that the Lord had brought on him."

Why is this curious? Because at first glance this would seem to negate the entire message of the book of Job. There are, however, at least two ways this verse can be understood to fit with the rest of the text. Job's relatives could have thought God was either *directly* or *indirectly* responsible for Job's suffering. Which one they believed would depend on their understanding of Satan's involvement in the situation.

First, Job's brothers, sisters, and acquaintances may have had no idea Satan was active behind the scenes, and so could have thought God attacked Job. It is a common occurrence throughout the book that people did not understand what was happening in Job's life (including Job himself), so they assumed God was directly responsible for his suffering.

Consider these instances:

• During Satan's first attack, one of Job's servants came to Job, announcing, "The fire of God fell from heaven and burned up the sheep and the servants and consumed them, and I alone have escaped to tell you."[126] *But the servant was mistaken. Satan had destroyed Job's possessions.*

• In response to Satan's first attack, Job said, "The Lord gave and the Lord has taken away."[127] *But Job was mistaken.* The Lord had given, and *Satan had taken away.*

• At the beginning of Satan's second attack, Job asked his wife, "Shall we indeed accept good from God and not accept adversity?"[128] *Job was wrong again. Satan had struck Job with boils.*

Who really ruined Job?

• Then the Lord said to Satan, "Behold, all that he has is in your power, only do not put forth your hand on him."[129]

• So the Lord said to Satan, "Behold he is in your power, only spare his life."[130]

• Then Satan went out from the presence of the Lord, and smote Job with sore boils from the sole of his foot to the crown of his head.[131]

Though Job and others around him may have thought God was responsible, the Bible clearly reveals it was Satan who attacked Job.

It is possible the Scriptures are simply recording what Job's relatives and friends *thought* was happening. They assumed, like the comforters, that God was responsible for Job's suffering. But if this is what they thought, then their assumptions were fallacious. In

---

[126] Job 1:16.
[127] Job 1:21.
[128] Job 2:10.
[129] Job 1:12.
[130] Job 2:6.
[131] Job 2:7.

this case, the Bible truly records what they understood about the suffering, but what they understood was truly mistaken. God did not attack Job.

Second, Job's relatives could have understood that another being, Satan, was involved in Job's experiences. If so, they may have believed God was involved indirectly, by allowing Satan to attack Job. In that case, though they did not believe God directly attacked Job, they may have assumed God was ultimately responsible because He "allowed" the suffering.

In talking about the idea of God's "allowing" something to happen, it is important to distinguish between two different definitions of the word "allow."[132] On the one hand, God could allow something to happen in that He is free, morally, to stop the event, but chooses not to do so. In this case, God would be responsible for the result. On the other hand, God must allow an event to take place because He is not free, morally, to prevent it. In this case, another moral being would be responsible for the result by virtue of putting God in a moral dilemma, hindering Him from preventing the result.

The first definition of "allow"—God could stop something from happening, but chooses not to do so—is rather hypothetical. When would God see something bad about to happen, being free morally to stop it, and then choose to let it happen anyway? This definition of "allow" is only possible if God has no moral law to which He submits. If God follows the law of love, then situations where God could stop evil, but chooses not to, would simply not exist. It would constitute committing evil by omission.[133] Even if God were to have some good reason for not stopping evil, He would still be guilty of "doing evil that good may come."[134] God's justice, goodness, and love would all be in question if He could respond to evil in this fashion.

As for the second definition, if someone walks up to another person on the street and shoots him, you could say God "allowed" that to happen. But in most cases like this, God cannot intervene

---

[132] Chapter 3 also contains a discussion of the definition and use of the word "allow."
[133] James 4:17.
[134] Romans 3:8.

without violating the free will of the perpetrator, so He must (in the moral sense) allow the attack.[135] It is this second definition of "allow" that applies to the case of Satan and Job. In this instance we can understand how Job's relatives could consider God ultimately responsible. He allowed the attack, but it is only because He was not morally free to prevent it.

Thus, when the text states Job's brothers and sisters consoled him over "all the evil that the Lord had brought on him," it is telling us their mistaken understanding of the situation, whether Satan was involved in their reasoning or not. It is true they believed this, but what they believed was not true.

The final verses of the Epilogue record how God restored Job's possessions, and his children, and then how his daughters were regarded as the fairest women in the land. Job died at 140, after seeing four generations of his descendants. He is portrayed in the end as an "old man and full of days." After all the drama in his life, one would think there would be a more amazing description of his final state. He was probably happy, though, to be finished with his suffering, and that the Lord was "full of compassion" and "merciful"[136] throughout his trials.

Lessons from the Book of Job

There are many lessons to learn from the story of Job. Here are a few of the things Job teaches us about God's moral relationship to evil:

• God respects the free will of all moral beings, including those who are in rebellion against Him, such as Satan. God's choice to make beings with a free will included a necessity on His part to respect the choices made by those beings.

• Living in love (disinterested benevolence) is crucial for the happiness of all moral beings under God's government. God wants all moral agents to live in love, since that will produce their highest well being.

---

[135] I say "most cases" because other agents could make choices to put God in a position morally to stop the evil. Please see my book *Why Pray?* for details on this form of agency.

[136] James 5:11.

• God uses the lives of those living in love to teach spiritual beings His wisdom. One way He does this is to contrast the behavior of a righteous person with the actions of the spiritual being.

• Since God respects the choices of all moral beings, God can be put into a moral dilemma by their choices. God brought this limitation on Himself when He created beings with a free will.

• God can be restricted in His actions by the wills of other moral agents. God may sometimes desire to do something for a moral being, but He can be hindered from doing that by the choices of the being. God wants all people to be saved. Yet God respects their free will so much, He would rather have the person suffer eternal torment in hell, than to violate their wills by forcing them to love Him.

• Truly innocent people can suffer because of the choices of other moral beings. God must allow this to happen when to stop the choices would cause greater harm than the suffering. The case of Job was one such case. Job suffered under the attack of Satan because of the importance of disinterested benevolence in God, and those who follow His example of living in love. Satan, by his choices, put God in a dilemma where He had to allow Satan to attack Job, even though that was not what God wanted.

Chapter 6

Logical and Practical Conclusions

The best preparation for suffering, or for helping others who are suffering, is to be armed with thoroughly biblical, intellectually satisfying answers for the problem of evil. If people have worked through this problem mentally before they suffer, then, when they do suffer, their questions will be more practical in nature, rather than relational. Instead of asking, "Oh God, why did you do this to me?" they are more likely to say, "I know God does not do things like this, so I need to figure out, if I can, why I am suffering as an innocent person. And if I can't uncover the source, at least I know it's not God's fault."

Logical Conclusions

There are two ways to state the logical conclusion concerning suffering—positively and negatively. It is really only one conclusion, but it can be phrased from the standpoint of those causing the suffering, or from God's perspective.

Positively stated, the conclusion looks like this:

All suffering of the innocent is directly or indirectly a result of wickedness in some finite moral agent.

Stated *negatively*, the conclusion looks like this:

No suffering of an innocent party can be attributed to God.

While some people might imagine innocent parties could suffer indirectly because of God's choices, this is a mistaken idea. If God must judge people for their sin, and if innocent parties are harmed in that judgment, the fault lies with the people who brought about the judgment, and not with God as the Judge.

When a man is incarcerated for stealing a car, whose fault is it he is in jail? Do we say it is the judge's fault? No, the man himself bears the responsibility, even though the judge sentenced the man to jail time. More to the point, if the prisoner's daughter misses her father because he is in jail, is it the judge's fault the girl is separated from her father? No, it is the criminal's fault. The child's grief is a consequence of her father's crime. Innocent people are often affected by a judge's sentencing of a guilty party, but in neither case is the suffering the responsibility of the judge.

The children who died in Sodom and Gomorrah were killed because of the sins of the adults in the city, not because of God. The same would be true of the children who died in Canaan under God's judgment carried out by the Israelites, though the children were sometimes spared.

Maybe a more pertinent example is how we all suffer daily because of choices people made before the flood. As the Moral Governor of the universe, God had to judge their actions, but we still suffer today as a result of their decisions. If people suffer in a natural disaster, they are suffering because of choices people made long ago to bring about the destruction of the earth. God is not the cause of the suffering. The people who prompted the judgment are responsible.

What can we conclude, then, concerning the basic reasons why innocent people suffer?

- God is not at fault when people intentionally harm other innocent people, such as in a mugging, a rape, or when a person persecutes another for preaching the Gospel.
- God is not at fault if an innocent person suffers because of disease or deformity. These happen because of the general effect of sin on the human body.
- God is not at fault when innocent people suffer in natural disasters. This happens because of the general effect of sin on the physical creation.

- God is not at fault when innocent people suffer because of an accident. These can happen because of the fallen state of the human race.
- God is not at fault when innocent people suffer under the attack of evil spiritual beings. This is due to free will, as with the malicious intent of other humans.
- God is not at fault in the suffering of the innocent when He does not intervene to stop the suffering. He is restricted by His own commitment to our freedom and significance to not interfere with our choices, or their consequences, unless He has some morally justified reason to do so.

In other words, God is not at fault when any innocent person suffers. God never intended there be any suffering or death. It is still not His intention that these things happen in the world He created. There is evil and suffering now because of the rebellion of finite moral agents (spiritual and human). And in the future, God will judge all evil, and create a new world where there is no suffering, pain, or death—only righteousness, peace, and joy.

Practical Conclusions

Logical answers to the problem of pain really should be considered when a person is not in the midst of suffering. Mental preparation is better handled before the person suffers, or after the emotional crisis of the suffering has passed. If a person tries to handle philosophical or theological questions about suffering in the midst of the pain, it is more likely the person will project any bitterness they have onto God, thus causing a conscious or subconscious strain in their relationship with the Lord. The situation itself is enough to endure. There is no need to possibly create more pain by forcing them to contemplate how God relates to their suffering.

As a matter of full disclosure, I should say that I learned this lesson the hard way, at the expense of a person I knew in my youth. She was in a car accident and had to spend many weeks in the hospital with a cast from her toes to the middle of her chest. During that time she asked me about how God related to her situation, and I tried to explain. The result of my efforts was that she projected the bitterness she had about the accident onto God, and her relationship with Him was severely damaged. I am not sure if she ever had a good relationship with God after that. I certainly hope she recovered.

It is true that I was young and inexperienced, but my lack of wisdom still caused another person terrible pain. I share this in the hope that every reader of this book will be more careful than I was, so we can spare other people unnecessary difficulties in their relationship with God.

The Negative Fruit of Misunderstanding

As noted elsewhere, when people lump all suffering together, they can cause confusion, and thus slander, or cause others to slander, God's character, particularly His justice. When possible, it is important to establish and separate the causes of suffering, in order to avoid accusing God of something for which He is not responsible. Otherwise, people can be affected negatively in their relationship with God, even to the point of not wanting to live for Him.

Consider the case of a pastor, who, when counseling a man born with no arms, said, "Well, we don't know why God wanted you to have no arms, but you need to trust Him. He must have a good reason to make you this way, so you just need to accept your situation."

"So God made me this way?" the young man asked.

"Yes. We might not understand why God did this, but since it is His will, you should accept it, trust Him, and get on with your life."

"Well, then," the counselee responded, "if God causes people to suffer like this, then I don't want anything to do with Him." At that, the counselee departed, left the church, and abandoned his faith.

If the pastor had only been properly informed about suffering, he could have strengthened the young man's faith, rather than driving him away from God. The idea that God planned all evil, or that all suffering is somehow His will, may seem to offer comfort to those who are suffering, but it does not take much thought to realize these views of suffering are more horrific than helpful.

Another of these unhelpful explanations is sometimes used when a person questions their value if they were born as a result of fornication, adultery, or rape. Someone tells them, "God planned every person who exists, and because God planned for you to exist, you have great value, and He has a purpose for your life."

While it is true that every human being is worth more than the whole world, and God has a purpose for each person, that does not mean God planned the existence of every individual. Because of their value, God committed Himself to loving them the same as every other person, starting from the moment they were conceived. Their value is determined by what they are as beings made in the image of God, and not by the sinful choices of their biological parents.

As for God's planning for every person to exist, if this were true, then it means God also had to plan the fornication, adultery, or rape that produced the pregnancy. This implies God is the author of evil, by guaranteeing that certain people will sin so other people can exist. But God has commanded us to abstain from all evil, and has told us that all sin is contrary to His will. Thus, He cannot be responsible for the fornication that results in the existence of a new human being.

Being Prepared with the Truth

"I want to thank you, Mike, for your teaching on apologetics, particularly your teaching on suffering." The young woman from my church had attended a week of teaching during the annual Vacation Bible School. When our church hosts this event, there are classes for all ages, and not just for the children. I had been asked to teach a week on apologetics to the high school and college age youth.

"Just two weeks ago, my grandfather, whom I loved very much, died suddenly," she explained. "We were all deeply sorry about his passing. But because of your teaching, I knew God never wanted anyone to suffer or die, so I knew God was not responsible.

It was a great comfort to know God did not take my grandpa from me."

It is impossible to place a value on this kind of preparation. It can mean the difference between a person's spiritual life and death. How many people have turned away from God because they mistakenly believed He was responsible for the suffering and death in the world? They usually will not be so blatant as to accuse God directly, but will question why God did not stop the suffering if He had the chance. But this is the same question. If He could have stopped it, but did not, then He is ultimately responsible for the suffering. But these kinds of questions do not plague the person who is prepared beforehand with the truth—the truth that God is not responsible for the suffering of any innocent party.

Understanding After Suffering

Even if people were not prepared mentally before they suffered, they can still find comfort in the truth after the emotional crisis of the suffering has subsided.

I was standing at the reception desk of a Christian community where I had been invited to speak for a week on apologetics. I noticed the receptionist seemed sad, so I asked what was wrong.

"My dad died recently of a heart attack," she responded. I think because she knew I was the guest speaker she ventured the question, "Why did God take my dad from me?"

"God did not take your dad from you," I said. "God never wanted anyone to die. That is why he told Adam and Eve not to eat from the tree. And He still does not like it when anyone dies, because it was never His will."

This helped some, but it was what the Holy Spirit did next that really answered her question. As I looked at her and prayed, I saw in my mind the image of a person smoking cigarettes. "Was your dad a chain smoker?" I asked.

"Yes," she said.

"And did he have heart disease?"

"Yes."

"And was his heart attack related to his heart disease?"

"Yes."

"So you see then, God did not want your dad to die. Your dad died because of his bad health habits." It was an amazing thing to see the answer register in her heart and on her face. The truth about her dad's death had brought her real peace. (Thank you, Holy Spirit.)

Now, not all situations are so easy to understand. The farther removed in space (geographically) and time (chronologically) the suffering is from the cause of the suffering, the harder it is to tell why any particular suffering is happening.

For questions like "Why was this baby born deformed?" we may never be able to pinpoint the exact reason why, but we do know the general reasons why. The world is fallen and corrupted because of the sin of the human race, and our bodies are not in the perfect condition of the original creation. This is why babies can be born deformed. God never wanted it, and still does not want it, but must allow it because He gave us free will, and had to allow us to destroy the earth, and our own bodies, if we so chose.

If we are convinced God is not responsible for the suffering of the innocent, it makes it so much easier to encourage people to trust God for His help in the midst of their suffering. Even if the information comes to them after the emotional crisis of the suffering is past, it can still help them maintain a good relationship with the Lord.

Helpful Actions and Attitudes During Suffering

Though each person's pain will be different, and each person's response to suffering will vary with their personality, circumstances, and relationships, there are some general actions and attitudes that can help during troubling times.

1. Do not assume God's guilt: It is amazing how people who want God to be fair with them can be completely unjust in their treatment of God when they are suffering. They will assume, usually because of bad teaching, that God is responsible for the suffering, even though they have absolutely no evidence this is the case. Yet we presume (in the United States, at least) a person is innocent until he is proven guilty. Why can't we at least do as much for God? It is unfair, and dishonest, to assign guilt to God for any suffering unless we have proof He is actually responsible. Of course, since He is not responsible for the suffering of any innocent party, this evidence will not be forthcoming. Rather, both logical and biblical evidence will prove God is not responsible.

2. If possible, try to uncover the reason for the suffering: People who do not press through to discover a possible reason for their suffering will often become bitter and resentful towards God. This can be conscious, or subconscious, but it will always cause a problem in the person's relationship with the Lord. The reason this happens is that "God" and the "reason for the suffering" can both be vague, unknown quantities, and the person's mind can sort both into the same mental category. God and the suffering then become associated with each other in the person's thinking, and any bitterness the person has about the suffering can be projected onto God. When possible, then, it is good to discover a reason for the suffering, and if a specific source is not found, at least a general reason for that type of suffering should explain the person's experience.

3. Repent of any bitterness, if necessary: When people suffer, they sometimes put themselves in a position morally where God cannot justly answer their questions.

Here is an example (quoted from my book *Why Pray?*) of how a person's attitude can affect how God responds to them.

When I was a missionary in Holland, one of the families in our mission group had a baby born with a heart defect. The baby lived for a few days, and then died from the defect. The parents were devastated from the loss, and all the rest of us could do was try to comfort them in their grief. Both parents became very withdrawn and quiet in their communications, but the father much more so than the mother.

One day I remembered I had told the father I would look something up in Greek and get back to him with an answer, and possibly a reference book to read. After I found the answer, I put a marker in the book, and carried the book to their house. The mother told me her husband was painting some walls in one of the dorm rooms as part of his afternoon chores.

I went to the room where he was painting, and since the window was open, I stood outside on the grass and told the man I had left the book with his wife. What happened next was quite a shock. The man began angrily asking me why his child had died. Why was God so cruel? Why didn't He do something to help the child? Why won't God talk to me when I pray? He went on for quite some time, which told me he had been doing a lot of thinking about his child's death.

As he was speaking, I prayed silently that God would help me answer this man. But what I heard from God was not what I was expecting. I thought God would give me some great pearl of wisdom to share, but no, He told me not to say anything at all. God told me to say nothing, and just walk away. "This can't be right," I thought. "He thinks God doesn't care for him. If I just walk away, he'll think I don't care about him either." But the impression was very strong—say nothing and walk away. So I did.

A couple of days later I saw the man in a meeting, and he asked if he could talk with me. I tried to prepare myself to hear from him what a horrible person I was, but that was not his attitude at all.

"I want to thank you, Mike, for walking away the other day."

Needless to say, I was more than shocked at his statement. "I don't understand," I said, "I thought you would be angry with me for leaving."

"Well, I was at first," he said, "but then I realized if you had said anything to try to answer my objections, I would have rejected what you said. You may have had a perfect answer to all my questions, but my heart was so bitter, I would not have responded correctly to anything. I would have resisted any truth you shared with me, and by doing that, I would have only condemned myself. I then realized what you did was the most loving thing you could do—you refused to talk with me. And that made me understand why God would no longer talk to me. As long as I was harboring bitterness in my heart, and was determined to reject anything God would say to me, it was the most loving thing for God to stop talking to me. He was silent because He loved me so much. He did not want to condemn me by telling me the truth, so He just said nothing. Since I have repented of my bitterness, and am willing to submit to whatever He tells me, God has started talking to me again. Thanks, Mike, for just walking away. God used you to show me why He was not talking with me."

I really did not know who was learning more in this situation. This was a living illustration of a very profound principle. When we are bitter against God, He will stop sharing His truth with us— not because He does not love and care for us, but precisely because He does. He will not condemn us with truth He knows our hearts are determined to reject, so in His love He waits silently until we are ready to listen again. What an amazing, wise, and loving Father we have.

So when we have questions about why an innocent person may be suffering, it is important to repent of any bitterness we might have, and open ourselves to God's explanation, whatever that may be. Otherwise, the Lord, in His great love for us, may go silent, waiting for a better time to show us the truth.

4. Affirm God's justice: What should people do while they are trying to discover the reason for their suffering? They should affirm the justice of God. The Lord declares of Himself that He is "just in all his ways, and kind in all His deeds." In the midst of suffering, a person might respond to God with statements like, "Thank you, God, that You never intended anyone should suffer or die. Thank You that You have always been just and kind in everything You have done. I don't know why I am suffering, but I do know it is not Your fault. Thank You for Your promise to never leave or forsake me. Please comfort me with the sense of Your presence and Your love during this time of trouble."

5. Where it is wise, seek the support of other people: Other people can be a great help, or a great hindrance to a suffering person. People who raise questions about God's goodness, or about the faith of the person, can increase the pain in a person's life.

When my wife became ill with endometriosis, and as a result had to have a hysterectomy, a visiting pastor was very wise and helpful in his advice.

"Don't you let anybody question your faith because you had this surgery. Somebody may try to accuse you of a lack of faith because this happened to you. But your faith is not in question here. This did not happen to you because of a lack of faith on your part. This kind of thing can happen just because we live in a fallen world. So don't let others question your faith, and don't you question your own faith. Just rest for now, get well, and trust God to love and comfort you during this time."

We really need more pastors like this who can minister comfort, faith, and strength to people in their time of need. And if you are suffering, seek out those who can minister to you in this way, avoiding those who speak discouragement and death with their tongues.

6. Do what you can to stop the suffering: There are two aspects of relieving suffering that must be kept in a delicate balance.

On the one hand, God is our primary relationship, so if we have questions about what to do, we should seek His guidance first. If He has wisdom for us, then that may solve the problem, and end our pain. Prayer for healing is one obvious avenue, but God can give supernatural wisdom, directing the sufferer to solutions he would not have imagined with his own finite mind.

On the other hand, God never wanted anyone to suffer, so we should have no problem using all godly means to stop the pain in our lives. This includes the whole scope of medical knowledge and treatment. They should be "godly" means, though, because in times of pain many occult healing practices might present themselves as options.

7. Beware of temptation to evil during a time of suffering: There is an interesting admonition Elihu gives to Job, when he warns, "Be careful, do not turn to evil, For you have preferred this to affliction." (Job 36:21) When people are in pain, they are often more vulnerable to temptation, or to attack by spiritual beings, than when they are well. Sometimes people will imagine that giving in to a particular temptation may bring them some comfort or release that would be preferable to the affliction they are experiencing. It is good, in times like these, to heed the admonition of Elihu, because giving in to sin will only add to a person's misery. It will not alleviate it.

8. Don't abandon good Christian disciplines: It is very easy to forget to pray, to praise God, to read the Bible, and to love our neighbor as ourselves when we are suffering. As far as it is possible and wise, these disciplines should continue, even though a person is in pain. Thanksgiving is also important, because it causes us to see what is good in our lives, even as the pain is clamoring for our attention. Remember, this is thanking God for who He is and what He does in the midst of our circumstances. It is not thanking God *for* the suffering, but thanking Him in the midst of suffering.

One summer, when my wife and I were in Spain, teaching at a Youth With A Mission center, I came down with a bad case of fever and dysentery. Unfortunately, the common toilets were on the other end of a very long building from where I was sleeping. To go to the bathroom, I had to walk the whole distance to the other end of the building, and then walk down two flights of stairs. I had made this trip many times during a long sleepless night.

One time, on my way back from the toilet, with my head in a fog from the fever, I realized I was not thanking God. Instead, I was concentrating solely on my own feelings. As I slowly trudged up the two flights of stairs, I tried to thank God for something with each step I climbed. When I reached the top of the stairs, I realized I had been healed. Now it still would have been right for me to give thanks to God, whether I was healed or not, but we never know, do we?

Some Things to Remember

Though we can talk about general principles related to the subject of suffering, there is no "generalized suffering." Each person's suffering is as personal and individual as the person himself. Every instance is different, and it would be a mistake to assume what works to help one suffering person will always help another. General principles are helpful, but they will only take us so far.

Also, when dealing with a suffering person, do not bring God into the conversation too soon, or too often. Discussing how God relates to the person's suffering may encourage the person to project onto God any bitterness they have about the incident, thus causing a problem in their relationship with the Lord.

Instead, try to comfort the person as best you can. As the Scriptures command us, "Weep with those who weep." When Job's friends saw his plight, they sat down with him in silence for a whole week. Just being with him, even in silence, was a sign of their true friendship.

Do not assume you will be able to help the person. God may have other people who can offer better support for this person at this time. You can offer your prayers, concern, and support without being directly involved with the person. Do not let your pride influence you to offer help when someone else may actually be able to do a better job.

And always keep in mind—as far as the suffering of the innocent is concerned, there just are no easy answers.

Appendix

Verses Using the Word "Incite" (Hebrew, *suth*)

Translations of the word are in ***bold italic***.

II Chronicles 18:31 - So when the captains of the chariots saw Jehoshaphat, they said, "It is the king of Israel," and they turned aside to fight against him. But Jehoshaphat cried out, and the LORD helped him, and God ***diverted*** them from him.

Deuteronomy 13:6 - "If your brother, your mother's son, or your son or daughter, or the wife you cherish, or your friend who is as your own soul, ***entice*** you secretly, saying, 'Let us go and serve other gods' …"

Job 36:16, 18 - "Then indeed, He ***enticed*** you from the mouth of distress, instead of it, a broad place with no constraint; and that which was set on your table was full of fatness. Beware that wrath does not ***entice*** you to scoffing; and do not let the greatness of the ransom turn you aside.

II Samuel 24:1 - Now again the anger of the LORD burned against Israel, and it ***incited*** David against them to say, "Go, number Israel and Judah."

I Chronicles 21:1 - Then Satan stood up against Israel and *moved* David to number Israel.

I Kings 21:25 - Surely there was no one like Ahab who sold himself to do evil in the sight of the LORD, because Jezebel his wife *incited* him.

Job 2:3 - And the Lord said to Satan, "Have you considered My servant Job? For there is no one like him on the earth, a blameless and upright man fearing God and turning away from evil. And he still holds fast his integrity, although you *incited* Me against him, to ruin him without cause."

Jeremiah 43:3 - but Baruch the son of Neriah is *inciting* you against us to give us over into the hand of the Chaldeans, so they will put us to death or exile us to Babylon.

II Chronicles 18:2 - Some years later he went down to visit Ahab at Samaria. And Ahab slaughtered many sheep and oxen for him and the people who were with him, and *induced* him to go up against Ramoth-gilead.

II Chronicles 32:15 - Now therefore, do not let Hezekiah deceive you or *mislead* you like this, and do not believe him, for no god of any nation or kingdom was able to deliver his people from my hand or from the hand of my fathers. How much less will your God deliver you from my hand?

II Chronicles 32:11 - Is not Hezekiah *misleading* you to give yourselves over to die by hunger and by thirst, saying, "The LORD our God will deliver us from the hand of the king of Assyria"?

II Kings 18:32b - But do not listen to Hezekiah when he *misleads* you, saying, "The LORD will deliver us."

Isaiah 36:18 - Beware that Hezekiah does not *mislead* you, saying, "The LORD will deliver us."

Jeremiah 38:22b - "Your close friends have *misled* and overpowered you; while your feet were sunk in the mire, they turned back."

Joshua 15:18 - It came about that when she came to him, she *persuaded* him to ask her father for a field. So she alighted from the donkey, and Caleb said to her, "What do you want?"

Judges 1:14a - Then it came about when she came to him, that she *persuaded* him to ask her father for a field.

I Samuel 26:19 - Now therefore, please let my lord the king listen to the words of his servant. If the LORD has *stirred* you *up* against me, let Him accept an offering; but if it is men, cursed are they before the LORD, for they have driven me out today so that I would have no attachment with the inheritance of the LORD, saying, 'Go, serve other gods.'

Bibliography

Brand, Dr. Paul, and Philip Yancey, *Pain: The Gift Nobody Wants*, (Diane Publishing: Darby, PA, 1999).

Buddhism, Information about the four noble truths and the eight-fold path found at - http://www.thebigview.com/buddhism/fourtruths.html.

Craig, Dr. William Lane, http://www.christianpost.com/news/atheist-says-hell-turn-christian-if-evil-is-explained-during-major-debate-89362/#VMqoAZLHyo8TMs9l.99.

Finney, Charles G., *Lectures on Systematic Theology,* (London: William Tegg and Co., 85, Queen Street, Cheapside, 1851).

Geddert, Tim. "Another Look at Romans 8:28." http://www.mbseminary.edu/files/download/geddert1.htm?file_id= 12815136

Hume, David, *Dialogues Concerning Natural Religion*, (Simon and Schuster: Parsippany, NJ, 1972).

Koukl, Gregory, *Augustine on Evil,* http://www.str.org/site/News2?page=NewsArticle&id=5124.

Lewis, C.S., *The Abolition of Man,* "Illustrations of the *Tao*," (New York: The MacMillan Company, 1969).

Lewis, C.S., *God in the Dock: Essays in Theology and Ethics*, ed. W. Hooper (Eerdmans: Grand Rapids, Michigan, 1970).

Lewis, C. S., *The Problem of Pain,* (The Macmillan Company: New York 1962).

Ramm, Bernard, *Protestant Biblical Interpretation* (Grand Rapids: Baker Book House, 1970).

Saia, Michael R., *Does God Know the Future?,* (Xulon Press: Fairfax, VA, 2002).

Saia, Michael R., *Understanding the Cross,* (Xulon Press: Fairfax, VA, 2007).

Saia, Michael R., *Why Pray?,* (Xulon Press: Fairfax, VA, 2014).

Zoroastrianism, Information about Ahura Mazda was derived from this website - http://www.farvardyn.com/zoroaster3.php - which appears to have been deactivated since that time.

Printed in the USA
CPSIA information can be obtained
at www.ICGtesting.com
LVHW041212180124
768654LV00008B/326